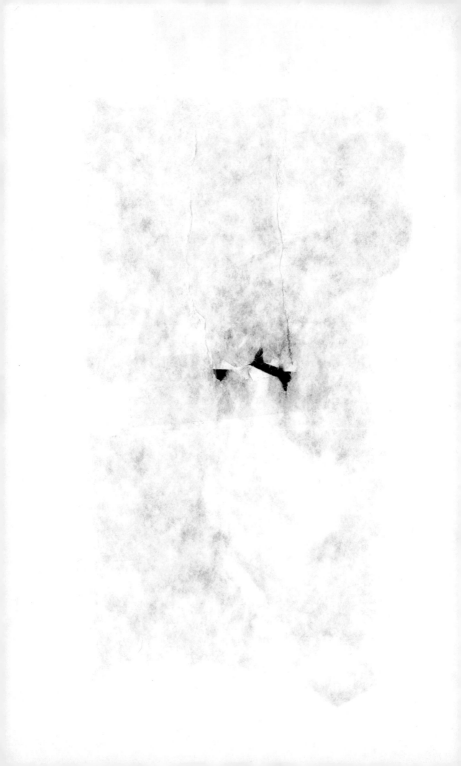

TWAYNE'S WORLD AUTHORS SERIES
A Survey of the World's Literature

FRANCE

Maxwell Smith
Guerry Professor of French, Emeritus
The University of Chattanooga
Former Visiting Professor in Modern Languages
The Florida State University

EDITOR

Eugène Fromentin

TWAS 640

EUGÈNE FROMENTIN

By EMANUEL J. MICKEL, JR.
Indiana University

TWAYNE PUBLISHERS
A DIVISION OF G.K. HALL & CO., BOSTON

Copyright © 1981 by G.K. Hall & Co.

Published in 1981 by Twayne Publishers,
A Division of G.K. Hall & Co.
All Rights Reserved

Printed on permanent/durable acid-free paper and bound
in the United States of America

First Printing

Library of Congress Cataloging in Publication Data

Mickel, Emanuel J., 1937–
    Eugène Fromentin.

    (Twayne's world authors series ; TWAS 640. France)
    Bibliography: p. 160
    Includes index.
    1. Fromentin, Eugène, 1820–1876—Criticism and interpreta-
tion.   I. Title.   II. Series: Twayne's world authors series : TWAS
640.   III. Series: Twayne's world authors series : TWAS 640.
France.
PQ2256.F5Z77   843'.8   81-4170
ISBN 0-8057-6484-4   AACR2

For my
Mother and Father

Contents

About the Author

Emanuel Mickel received his B.A. from Louisiana State University and his M.A. and Ph.D. from the University of North Carolina. He has taught at the University of Nebraska and since 1968 has been at Indiana University, where he has taught graduate work in medieval studies as well as the nineteenth-century novel and poetry. Mr. Mickel was promoted to professor in 1973, served as Associate Dean of the Graduate School from 1976 to 1978, and has been the Director of the Medieval Studies Institute since 1976.

Professor Mickel has been active as a scholar in both medieval and nineteenth-century studies. His books include *The Artificial Paradises in French Literature* (1969), *Marie de France* (1974), and the projected nine volume edition of *The Old French Crusade Cycle*, Vol. I, *La Naissance du Chevalier au Cygne* (with Professor Jan Nelson) (1977). He has published more than thirty articles in American, French, German, and Italian periodicals. Over the years he has received a number of grants and is currently (1979–81) funded by NEH to produce a translation and commentary (with Professor Denis Sinor) of Hayton's *La Flor des Estoires de la Terre d'Orient*. In 1981–82 he will hold the Lilly Open Fellowship, a position that will permit a year's leave from teaching to study legal questions pertaining to Old French Literature.

Preface

In this slender volume I have tried to provide the student and scholar with an interesting general introduction to Eugène Fromentin and his works. Although the Twayne Series is devoted to literature, I felt that chapters on Fromentin's other works would be useful to the reader who wished to assess the artist's place in the nineteenth century and would contribute to an understanding of the novelist and his art. After a concise account of his life and career in chapter 1, chapters 3, 4, and 5 provide brief introductions to Fromentin's work as a painter, author of travel books, and art critic. Because Fromentin's aesthetic perspective played such a significant role in every facet of his literary and artistic production, I dealt with this question in chapter 2 before treating his works. Aesthetic questions also arise and are discussed in subsequent chapters, however.

In the last six chapters the focus is on basic questions regarding the novel. Chapter 6 includes a brief discussion of the sources which may have influenced Fromentin, a summary of the action and, because the novel is largely autobiographical, identifies the fictional characters with their alleged models. In chapter 7 an attempt was made to examine various ways the text might be organized for analysis and chapter 8 develops one of the major themes of the book, the quest for self-knowledge. Chapter 9 concerns the roles of the principal characters and Fromentin's use of psychology and chapter 10 focuses on some of the artistic techniques which Fromentin used in creating an effective novel. Unfortunately a number of interesting ideas and suggestions had to be omitted because of limited space. In the case of Fromentin's literary style, the excellent studies of Barbara Wright and Arthur Evans made it possible to omit any study of this aspect of Fromentin's art in this book. Finally, the bibliography had to be limited to only the more important and accessible works. For an extensive bibliography through 1972, the reader is referred to the excellent work of Barbara Wright.

I wish to thank the Interlibrary Loan Department of the Indiana University Library for its help in obtaining many items which would have been unavailable to me otherwise and I am indebted to the Office of Research and Graduate Development for their generous financial assistance. I am also grateful to my wife and family for their patience and encouragement.

EMANUEL J. MICKEL, JR.

Indiana University

Chronology

1870   Trip to Venice cut short by beginning of Franco-Prussian War.
1874   Third edition and important preface of *Un Eté dans le Sahara* published by Lemerre.
1875   Trip to Belgium and Holland.
1876   Publication of *Maîtres d'autrefois* in the *Revue des Deux Mondes*. Appears as book with Plon.
1876   Death of Fromentin on 27 August.

CHAPTER 1

Fromentin's Artistic Career

I *Childhood and Adolescence*

IN SOME WAYS it is extraordinary that Eugène Fromentin, painter, novelist, and art critic, one of the few artists ever to be successful in three different disciplines, should have been born in La Rochelle to a staunch bourgeois family whose reputation in business, law, and civil service dated back several hundred years. The philosophical, religious, and social ideas associated with the Protestant stronghold represent the antithesis of what nineteenth- and twentieth-century scholars would consider the ideal milieu for the cultivation of artistic originality. And there is a strong sentiment among critics that the restrictive atmosphere of Fromentin's family and the aesthetic values of his father hampered the development of the young painter's techniques and stifled the creative imagination of the future novelist. One must realize that such criticism has its own bias and is based on a particularly modern notion of the role of imagination in the creative process. It is a perspective which sees imitation as the antithesis of the creative impulse. The narrow focus on originality in form and matter stems from the social and intellectual upheaval which has marked post-eighteenth-century Europe. Although influenced strongly by Romantic attitudes and values, Fromentin's artistic roots reach back to an earlier system of aesthetic values, so that he represents an interesting amalgam of Romantic and Classic traits.

Fromentin was born on 24 October 1820, to a family which might be classified as being among the aristocracy of the bourgeoisie. The statement is not so anomalous as it might seem. One of the outstanding characteristics mentioned by most who knew Fromentin well was his aristocratic bearing, his sense of restraint and good taste. A quiet dignity and distinguished manner marked his personality. Modest about his own work and gentle in his comments about the work of others, Fromentin was, nonetheless, highly critical of his own artistic efforts and accepted only the highest quality.

Although Fromentin's ancestors had been of the Huguenot persuasion in the sixteenth century, the recent family was Catholic. Fromentin's mother was especially devout and serious by nature and played a large role in the artist's life. Because of her reserve she was perceived as an intimidating figure; in reality she was a sensitive, pious woman, devoted to the family and to the children's education. More importance should be given to Fromentin's philosophical-theological background, despite the fact that his own religious interest seems to have been limited to that of the ordinary practicing Catholic. Even though he was not pious or devout, Fromentin's ethical perspective was firmly rooted in the traditional Pauline-Augustinian theology which was the keystone of European Catholicism until relatively recent times and was still particularly influential among Huguenots and conservative, provincial Catholics.

If Fromentin's mother influenced his upbringing, his father played a major role in his artistic career. A well-known medical doctor of the area who was director of the *maison d'aliénation* for many years, Dr. Fromentin was a serious, energetic, and learned man. However, because he resisted Eugène's career as an artist, what must have been another side to him is rarely presented. Friends knew him not as the stern father who insisted that his son study law, but as a rather witty, kindly man with pleasant personality traits. It is frequently noted that Dr. Fromentin was himself an amateur painter of landscapes; however, he is strongly criticized for lacking talent and for being a student of Bertin and follower of the academic school of landscape painting. Nonetheless, despite the lack of sympathy among critics, one must acknowledge that he was a man of considerable breadth of interest, intelligence, and talent and that Fromentin's debt to his father must have been large.

In school the young Eugène was a splendid student in every subject, excelling especially in Greek and Latin and earning many firsts in the rigorous nineteenth-century French educational system. As a youngster he enjoyed his summers at the family home at Saint Maurice just a few miles from La Rochelle. A sensitive youth, he was drawn to the severity of the coastal landscape and always expressed a love for autumn and an appreciation for solitude. His portrayal of light on the African desert, which some see as a transposition of the light from his own region, impressed certain critics for its accuracy at a time when a tradition of brilliant, bright hues had become established. During his summer vacations he became the companion of Jenny Léocadie Chessé, a creole girl nearly four years older than he. In 1834, just when Fromentin began to have a sense of his feelings for her, Jenny married Emile Béraud, an event which later played a central role in his only novel.[1] Fromentin continued to visit Jenny regularly for several years, eventually recognizing that his affection for her extended beyond what had once been childhood friendship. The relationship developed between Jenny and Eugène to the point where Fromentin's family interceded and sent him to Paris to begin his study of the law.

II *Fromentin in Paris*

In November 1839 Fromentin left La Rochelle and took up residence with his brother, Charles, in Paris. It was a difficult period of transition for the young law student, who, in the early months, often remained alone. His friends noticed that he ate too little and was unusually thin, even for his own size. For some time he was depressed about his unhappy romance and his separation from Jenny. He gradually resumed his friendship with Emile Beltrémieux, whom he had met in La Rochelle. Beltrémieux, who was two years older than Eugène, had an important formative influence on his younger friend. Like Fromentin's brother, Charles, Beltrémieux was a student of medicine, but he was also keenly interested in literature, history, poetry and the social questions of the day. Beltrémieux's sister, Lilia, who was interested in painting and corresponded with Fromentin on the subject, apparently developed a romantic attachment for him and may have served as the mysterious chaperon during his visits to Jenny Béraud.

During this period Fromentin was introduced to a religious, literary circle where he met Paul Bataillard, a law student four years older than he and destined to leave law to pursue his scholarly interests at the Ecole des Chartes. Bataillard was especially interested in the influence of religion on social and political issues and pursued his studies of religion, philosophy, and politics. In these early years Fromentin shared Bataillard's ardent republican leanings and they became good friends. For some time he was probably Fromentin's closest friend, the person with whom he shared his most personal thoughts.

While pursuing his legal studies, Fromentin showed a definite inclination toward a literary career. Michelet and Quinet taught at the Sorbonne and Fromentin attended their lectures. Although he continued to sketch and paint, having learned the rudiments from his father, he was more interested in literary composition. He wrote much poetry (very little of which survives) modeled on Lamartine, Sainte-Beuve, and Chénier. With Bataillard he began a study of Quinet's forgotten epic, *Ahasverus*.[2]

During the winter of 1842–43 Fromentin passed his exams and entered an apprenticeship in the office of M. Denormandie. At this time his career and interest shifted from literature to painting. Reluctantly his father agreed to allow him to pursue his avocation by entering the studio of Rémond (1795–1875), a painter associated with the academic school of landscape painting. After several months Fromentin left Rémond and entered the studio of Louis Cabat (1812–1893), an important proponent of the realistic landscape. Cabat especially studied the Dutch school and was fascinated by the English painters Constable and Gainsborough. Because Cabat opposed the academic school and sought to bring the painter to a more direct and realistic imitation of nature, Fromentin's defection from Rémond could not have pleased his father, who had selected Rémond's studio personally.

III   *Fromentin and Algeria*

Fromentin was early drawn to the nascent school of realistic landscape painting and especially to the Orientalists Marilhat[3] and Decamps. In 1845 he sent two articles to the *Revue Organique* concerning the Salon of 1845. One can see his ideas reflected even in this early criticism and in the painters he chose to discuss: the Orientalists Delacroix, Decamps, and Marilhat and painters from the modern school of landscape painting, Cabat, Daubigny, Corot, Rousseau, and Dupré.

In 1846 he was offered the opportunity to make a trip to Algeria in the company of another young painter, Charles Labbé, and Armand du Mesnil, a friend from Paris who would play a large role in Fromentin's development and who remained a lifelong friend. Because his parents were still hostile to his growing interest in pursuing an artistic career and because he did not wish to worry his mother concerning the voyage, Fromentin did not tell his parents that he was leaving for Algeria. He gave Bataillard letters to send to his mother in an effort to make her think that he was still in Paris.[4] The young painter was in search of a subject matter he could call his own. He sensed an affinity for North Africa and felt that here was a wonderful opportunity to acquaint himself with the area. The importance of the trip to him can be seen in the uncharacteristic subterfuge and resistance to his family's wishes. Fromentin was sensitive to his mother's personality and took great pains not to hurt her even when his own needs ran contrary to her wishes. And although he was resolute in following his artistic career, he never ceased in his attempts to persuade his father and mother that his choice of career was reasonable and worthy of support, this despite long years of resistance, frustration, and considerable financial hardship.

Fromentin left Marseilles on 10 March 1846, and returned six weeks later in mid-April. While in North Africa he visited not only the heavily French-oriented cities of Algiers and Blida,[5] but he also made brief trips to Medea, Miliana, and Kolea in an effort to experience the life of the Arab in a more natural setting. The trip was decisive in Fromentin's career. He returned with many sketches and studies of what he had seen, material that sparked his interest and became the subject matter of future paintings.

Once back in Paris the young painter took up residence near du Mesnil and became a close friend of the family. In the course of the year he spent time in Normandy with Labbé and at La Rochelle with his parents. He was painting under the influence of Cabat and Marilhat and realized that he must become better acquainted with North Africa if he were ever to develop a style of his own. By the summer of 1847 he had reached a low point in his work, depressed and unable to paint. In August he wrote to his father explaining his need to return to Africa. Although he valued imitation of the masters, he felt that he had to experience the nature which he was striving to create and attempted to persuade his father of the trip's benefit.

In September Fromentin again left Marseilles, this time accompanied by the painter, Auguste Salzmann, in addition to his former companion, Charles Labbé. During the autumn of 1847 Fromentin spent time in Algiers and at Blida, where he painted the *rue des marchands*. Much to his chagrin he learned that one of his closest friends, Emile Beltrémieux, had died. Both Emile's mother and Lilia reproached Fromentin for his absence, a situation which grieved and frustrated him.

In January Fromentin sought again to escape French influence and traveled by boat to Philippeville with Auguste Salzmann, a crossing that turned out to be more dangerous than anticipated. From there he made the arduous and fascinating journey into the desert to Constantine, Biskra, and Sidi Okba, a journey which he considered most successful from every standpoint. At Biskra he learned of the abdication of Louis-Philippe and was urged by his family to return to France. Despite his reluctance to leave the desert he had come to love, Fromentin began his return in April and arrived in Marseilles in late May 1848.

Back in La Rochelle Fromentin found it difficult to adjust to the routine of his parent's home. They were still opposed to his career and he felt ill at ease and a stranger in the community. By September he was miserable about the lack of progress in his own work and complained bitterly about the monotony of his life. To him the atmosphere was stifling and the solitude unbearable. Du Mesnil attempted, but without notable success, to intervene with Fromentin's parents on his behalf. In November Fromentin left La Rochelle to return to Paris to live with the du Mesnil family.

The Salon of 1849, to which Fromentin sent five paintings, was a great success for the young painter. It served to impress his father, who became slightly less hostile to his son's career.[6] Eugène himself was greatly encouraged by the sale of some of his paintings. He longed for the day when he would no longer be financially dependent on his parents. Although he was far from such independence, he had caught the attention of critics and painters and he could see the possibility of a steady income from his work. Fromentin's own probity and high standards, however, worked against his becoming financially self-sufficient. Not only did he suffer periods when he was unable to work satisfactorily, but he destroyed three-fourths of the work which he managed to complete. Like Baudelaire, Fromentin believed that the artist must be his own monitor and permit only his best work to survive as an example of his ability.

Although he had trouble painting during the winter of 1850, he had eleven paintings accepted at the Salon and was greatly encouraged by the recognition he was receiving. In January and February of 1851 he was at La Rochelle. Despite the feeling that he was out of place among his family and in his home town, he nonetheless appreciated the softening in his father's attitude toward his career and looked to the future with optimism. One senses in his letters that he was beginning to feel the self-assurance brought by success and recognition.

For some time a close affection had been growing between du Mesnil's niece, Marie Cavellet de Beaumont, and Fromentin.[7] Marie was considerably younger than Eugène, yet one finds brief references to her in his correspondence, mostly in the form of one wishing to be remembered to a member of the family. Marie had developed a strong attachment for her uncle's friend and nearly despaired that Fromentin would ever share her feelings. In spite of the reticence of his personality, Fromentin made his feelings known in the spring of 1851. He began to see that his career as an artist might provide enough income to support a wife and family. After a brief conflict with his parents over his proposed early date for their marriage, Fromentin acquiesced to his parents' will and the couple was married in May 1852.

Fromentin did not participate in the Salon of 1852, because he hoped to display his new work. For some months afterward he worked diligently but was unable to produce anything significant. He believed that he must make yet another trip to North Africa to provide him with the material for new work. In the autumn of 1852 he and his wife departed for Algeria. Fromentin remained at Mustapha until February 1853, hoping to paint from his observation point there rather than seeking out remote areas as in the past. In the spring of 1853 he spent two months at Blida with the Labbé family and, once du Mesnil had brought him the necessary funds to continue his stay, spent two months in the hottest part of the summer at Laghouat and at Aïn-Mahdy, a remote village not among the French possessions and never before visited by a European painter. In August he was back at Blida and in October Marie and he returned to France.

IV *Travel Literature and Novel*

Because Fromentin painted better from memory than he did while observing his subject first hand, his finished product from the year in North Africa was slight. He had a splendid ability to recall detail and, as will be seen later, painting from memory suited his aesthetic ideas. To help him remember he sketched a great deal and kept a journal during his stay. In the years immediately following Fromentin was chagrined by his lack of funds and his continuing dependence on his family. He received little from the middlemen who purchased his paintings and then resold them for twice the sum. Moreover, his work was not quite commanding the same attention or being so warmly received as a few years earlier. Thus, the birth of a daughter in 1854 and continuing financial distress made him decide to publish the journal he had kept while in North Africa. During the summer of 1856 he prepared *Un Eté dans le Sahara*, material drawn from the two months spent in the Sahara. The text first appeared in the *Revue de Paris* and was then published as a volume by Lévy. Although the work was not immediately popular, it received rave notices from critics and soon became one of the favorite travel books on North Africa. The *Revue des Deux Mondes* approached him about writing a sequel. Because of an illness he worked on the remainder of his journal, *Une Année dans le Sahel*, only intermittently for the next months. The text was published in late 1858 and was followed again by a volume with Lévy, which was bought up immediately.

Meanwhile, his showing at the Salon of 1859 was warmly received and he earned a first-place medal. Despite his success, however, he was still having financial problems. The director of the *Revue des Deux Mondes*, François Buloz, had suggested that Fromentin write a novel. Fromentin began to work on the project in 1859, but he was slowed by illness and the difficulties of the task. As much a perfectionist in writing as in painting, Fromentin composed the text very slowly and revised it over and over. Moreover, the subject matter, a fictional version of his own earlier romance with Jenny Léocadie Chessé, was difficult for him to express. Finally, the book appeared in the 15 April, 1 May, and 15 May 1862 issues of the *Revue des Deux Mondes*. The work was not well received by the public at large, but it immediately drew high praise from some of the most respected names of the period. Flaubert wrote that he had not been able to put the novel down and had read it in one sitting. Sainte-Beuve spoke well of the novel and George Sand, with whom Fromentin had been corresponding,[8] was very enthusiastic about the book, especially praising it for its portrayal of places and people and for the profundity of analysis. Nonetheless, she suggested several changes before publishing the novel in book form. Among other things she urged Fromentin to provide a transition between the despair of his final separation from Madeleine and his happiness of later years. She felt that the reader should be more prepared for the change in events.

Furthermore, she did not like the attempted suicide of Olivier where it occurs. Fromentin wrote that he would make the corrections. In the end he did not alter the book significantly and it was published in January 1863 by Hachette. Subsequently that text gained in popularity and saw more than thirty printings by the early years of the twentieth century and has maintained its status to this day.

In general the decade of the 1860s was good to Fromentin, who had become known for his work in three different areas of artistic endeavor. At the Salon of 1863 he exhibited three of his most celebrated canvases and sold several paintings in the following year. Socially he was much in demand during these years, spending much time with Gustave Moreau, Alexander Bida, and Charles Busson. He even accepted an invitation from the Emperor and Empress to visit Compiègne in the autumn of 1864.

Still his success was not entire. He stood for the seat made vacant at the death of Picot on the Académie des Beaux-Arts, but was unsuccessful.[9] In 1869 he was a member of the French delegation sent to Egypt for the inauguration of the Suez Canal. During the rushed trip he visited Alexandria, Cairo, and the Upper Nile. Although he had little time to paint or sketch, he managed to keep a notebook. Fromentin never redrafted the work into a travel book, but the notebook has been published by Louis Gonse at the end of his study of the painter.

Fromentin was not completely happy about his work in this period. He began to feel trapped by the Oriental subject matter which had given him his recognition as an artist. Because of his aesthetic perspective, it had mattered little to him early in his career what the external subject was. He felt that this did not limit his expression in that his treatment of man transcended the outer trappings. Yet his own presentation of the Near East led critics and viewers to expect a certain kind of Orientalism from him and it became clear that they were unwilling to accept work which seemed beyond his "specialty." At the 1868 Salon he exhibited *Arabes attaqués par une lionne* and *Centaures et Centauresses s'exerçant à tirer de l'arc*. In general the first of these paintings received high praise, while the second was severely criticized for not being in his manner. Only Odilon Redon praised Fromentin for what he saw as a rare combination of fantasy and realism.

Fromentin traveled to Venice with his friends Busson and Bataillard in June of 1870, a trip cut short by the sudden outbreak of hostilities and the disastrous French defeat. He returned to La Rochelle and followed the events of the summer and autumn with growing consternation and grief. Optimistic assessments of the French military situation were followed by news of unexpected defeat in unimagined proportions. Fromentin was deeply grieved by the humiliation of the French loss and bitterly resented the monarchies of Europe, which he blamed for the disaster. In 1872, after the end of the war and the revolution, he exhibited two paintings from his trip to Venice at the Salon. Once again the works were coldly received. The Orientalist's Venice did not match the traditional image of the city found in the painting of the period. Fromentin was in a rather difficult situation. Some were saying that his Oriental work was no longer new and tended to restate what he had already done. Yet his attempts to move into new subject matter were rejected because it represented a radical departure in subject and style from his best-known work.

V   The Final Years

In what were to be the final years of his life, Fromentin did not enter his work frequently in the exhibitions. He did not participate in the 1873 and 1875 showings and exhibited only two paintings in 1874. Finally, in 1876, he exhibited the two Nile paintings which stemmed from his Egyptian trip. These were better received than his other departures from Algeria, perhaps because the subject was still North Africa and not considered foreign to his work.

The years since 1848 had marked a gradual but major change in Fromentin's perspective. It is reflected in the dispute and break with his old friend Paul Bataillard, whose political views were now sufficiently different from Fromentin's to make their continued friendship difficult. Prior to 1848 both young men had been ardent republicans, liberals, and humanitarians to the left of center politically. The abortive revolution of 1848 caused many artists and writers to turn from politics in disgust and disillusionment. After 1848 Fromentin gradually became more conservative in his opinions and considered his youthful views to be more fanciful and idealistic than politically realistic. Bataillard, who had become a Protestant liberal, saw Fromentin's shift in views as a kind of aristocratic dilettantism, though Fromentin's ideas had really only crystallized within a provincial, Catholic framework.

This shift is noticeable in related areas. In the early years Fromentin's interest in the Orientalism of the Marilhats and Decamps, with the emphasis on Realism rather than traditional presentation, marked him as a painter of the new school. However, the continuing trend toward Realism in the work of Courbet or Millet went beyond what Fromentin's aesthetic values could tolerate. Realism in the sense of the objective realism of a Courbet seemed to miss the point of art to Fromentin. And he certainly had little taste for the further shift by Manet and the "new" generation.

One might see this problem as the essence of his novel, *Dominique*, with its repudiation of Romanticism in favor of the Classical ideal. Although Realism is not rejected, it is understood within an aesthetic framework which emphasizes the author's responsibility to capture an object's essential reality rather than its objective shape:

Le décalque mécanique d'un objet, par exemple la photographie, nous fixera-t-il mieux sur la réalité de cet objet? Que nous apprendra-t-il sur l'essence même du réel? Rien de plus, puisque, étant l'objet lui-même, la difficulté de se prononcer sur le caractère absolu des choses se reproduit à propos de l'image, comme elle existe à propos de l'objet.[10]

Fromentin reedited his *Sahara* and *Sahel* in the autumn of 1874 and wrote an important preface for the two works. The winter of 1875 was difficult for the painter because of poor health, which prevented his painting much of the time. For years he had been taking notes with a view toward writing some art criticism. In 1875 du Mesnil persuaded him to turn his full attention to the subject. Beginning in July he made a trip alone to Belgium and Holland where he visited museums and churches which contained paintings of the Flemish and Dutch masters. As was his custom, he took copious notes concerning each painting and then reworked the materials into book form after his return. It was a difficult task for the scrupulous Fromentin, because he found that his own appreciation for Rembrandt, while great, did not match the acclaim which tradition accorded his work. His integrity forced him to reflect this attitude in his criticism, yet his modesty made him doubt his judgment. Fromentin agonized over the problem and sought to understand why his perception contradicted the accepted values. In the end he had to accept his evaluation and he published his *Maîtres d'autrefois* in the *Revue des Deux Mondes* between 1 January and 15 March 1876. The text drew much attention from the press and was widely read and much discussed. Today the volume is accepted as one of the finest pieces of art criticism produced in the nineteenth century. It is especially admired for the candor displayed by the author and for the technical expertise he could call upon in discussing the works of art.

Shortly after this last work Fromentin was taken by a sudden illness.[11] After four brief days of fever he died, only fifty-six years of age at the time, hardly an old man by modern standards. It is interesting to speculate what he might have done had he lived another twenty years. In some ways his artistic career had reached an impasse. Orientalism was waning and his style was not likely to gain him favor with critics when turned to new subject matter. Contrarily his literary career might well have flourished. It is not likely, I think, that he would have written another novel. The motivation for his first was so personally oriented. He may well have written more art criticism, however, especially of historically established schools of art where the question of modern taste and politics was not at issue. Given the quality of *Maîtres d'autrefois,* it is a pity that our speculation did not have the opportunity to become a reality.

CHAPTER 2

Fromentin's Aesthetic

I *Romantic and Classic*

G IVEN the fact that Fromentin was heavily influenced by Romanticism and was the author of a confessional novel, one might
expect him to be among those espousing Romantic aesthetic values.
Many writers and painters of the period had turned from Neoclassical
artistic principles, which they perceived as codified rules hampering
personal inspiration. The rebellion against the state, social structures, and the forms and rules associated with Neoclassicism in art
was widespread in the early nineteenth century and led to numerous
manifestos which denounced Neoclassicism and proclaimed freedom
in the arts regarding subject matter and form. Because of restrictions
of taste and the basic tenet that the concern of art should be Beauty,
Neoclassical art avoided subjects, conduct, or language generally
considered in bad taste. As part of their program of liberation, many
Romantic writers deliberately chose subjects which they felt had
been neglected by art and treated them in a style and language which
violated the Neoclassical canon. One of the standard charges made
against Neoclassical art was that it neglected any true historical
context. Whether dealing with ancient Greece, Persia, or the Otto-
man Empire, its characters remained French in psychology and it
treated only superficially, and by no means accurately, the setting and
history of the text.

One of the interesting aspects of the movement toward Realism,
which the concern for historical accuracy fostered, is that many of the
artists who painted or wrote in a realistic vein retained, nonetheless,
a strong flavor of Neoplatonic thought in their philosophical perspective. Fromentin's own conservative, Catholic background oriented
him toward the philosophical position found in the Augustinian tradition, itself heavily influenced by the Greek notion that the world in
which we live is only a reflection of Reality, and that the world which

men call real is really only an enigma which obscures the relationship between the world of form and substance. Traditionally the poet was perceived as a seer who penetrated the reality of life, divined the essence of that reality, and created a work of art which revealed and communicated that essence to other human beings. Fromentin had a number of Romantic leanings, but he always set them aside when they conflicted with the basic assumptions of his aesthetic and philosophical view.

Thus it is natural that Fromentin should be so preoccupied with permanence and that Dominique should attempt to discover the essence of his own nature. Fromentin loved both the solid, unchanging nature of the desert and its impenetrable reaches. In the immovable surface of the desert, despite the superficial modifications wrought by the different seasons, one can see an image of life itself. Time and fortune cause ephemeral changes but the underlying, absolute values remain constant. Contrarily the sea was not appreciated by Fromentin. Its continuously fluctuating surface and turbulent depths remind one of the impermanence of existence, the constant variation precipitated by the imperfection of form and nature. It also explains why Dominique disliked the spring of the year, a time of tribulation and transformation in the novel, and why he preferred the quiet peace of autumn. Marie Eckstein sees in Dominique's passion and love for sensation a threat to the continuity of his being.[1] When Dominique spends the summer with Madeleine at Trembles, Eckstein suggests that he is attempting to ". . . apprivoiser la passion en transformant l'être aimé en un autre lui-même."[2] By associating his passion with his past, he is attempting to integrate his love into the substance of his permanent being. She sees a struggle between continuity and discontinuity in the novel represented by the conflict between Augustin and Olivier. Olivier lives in constant, expansive activity, attempting to escape ennui through the gratuitous pleasures of the present moment. In Olivier's disfigurement ". . . Fromentin détruit délibérément l'extérieur d'un homme qui n'a que trop vécu à l'extérieur de lui-même. . . . "[3] Augustin represents Dominique's attempt to establish the permanence and continuity of his own being.

His quest to know himself for what he really is derives, then, from his interest in the essence of things as opposed to the activity of things in life. Thus he is less interested in whether or not he could be successful as a poet or writer than in whether he has the talent to create works of permanent value. Fromentin's philosophical perspective influenced his aesthetic values and determined his attitude toward Realism. Ultimately it caused him to reject the values of Romanticism, even though his own personal sensibilities caused him to share many Romantic aspirations and have great sympathy for the Romantic temperament.

II *Fromentin and Realism*

Certain aspects of Fromentin's career and work reflect a concern for Realism which might lead the casual reader astray. Certainly among the vanguard of painters classified as Romantic in the 1830s was the work of the Orientalists, chiefly Delacroix, Marilhat, and Decamps. To be sure Romantic writers and painters were fascinated by the exotic Near East and North Africa, both areas recently opened to the French artist by the government's active role in these regions. However, most of the painters who followed the French were scarcely concerned about the realistic detail of their paintings in terms of costume, values, or historical accuracy. In time a certain stylistic expectancy grew up surrounding the Oriental painting, but the three mentioned above came to be recognized for their attempt at greater fidelity in reproducing North African costumes and mores.

None of the artists in question had spent much time abroad and the young Fromentin felt that there was great opportunity to contribute significantly as an Orientalist. He had begun study in the studio of M. Rémond, a recognized painter and teacher of the academic style of painting. Although Fromentin did not disagree with some of the basic premises of this school and certainly agreed with the need for imitation of the masters, he nonetheless felt out of place with Rémond and gained the reluctant permission of his father to enter the studio of Louis Cabat, a painter closely associated with the modern trend toward Realism. When Fromentin wrote to his father and mother to explain his need to go to Africa, he emphasized that he must observe life among the Arabs if he hoped to be successful as a painter of North African scenes. On October 4, 1847, he writes to Bataillard:

. . . je veux pénétrer profondément dans l'intimité de ce peuple. . . . C'est le menu détail de la vie domestique, des usages, des coutumes, que je veux apprendre; je veux que tout cela me devienne aussi familier que notre vie européenne.[4]

On the face of it the quotation could come from a painter or writer of the growing school of Realism with its emphasis on the "menu détail." However, the key to understanding his point of view is the phrase "pénétrer profondément dans l'intimité." As he writes further on in the letter, ". . . c'est le côté poétique et intime des choses qui me frappe et que je veux saisir."[5] Fromentin wishes to know everything he can learn about the Arab in his natural environment, so the details of history, costume, setting, and custom are important for coming to understand the character of the Arab. His intent is not to present unusual or bizarre scenes so as to pique the curiosity or amaze the European reader. His purpose is to capture the essential character of the North African Arab, to understand him as a man, as he relates to all men, but also to isolate those qualities which distinguish him.

Fromentin discourses at length on his attitude toward Realism in art in his discussion with Louis Vandell over the latter's drawing of geological formations. Vandell is annoyed when Fromentin does not recognize the area represented in his sketches. His point is that they are so accurately drawn that anyone should know them at once. Fromentin uses the opportunity to distinguish between copying nature and revealing its essential features. Vandell's drawings lack the color, shading, and perspective which capture the basic characteristics that make something what it is. Although the art of the great masters is realistic in appearance, one must not be deceived as to their intent. When they added color or emphasized certain details it was not to remain faithful to the scene itself but to reveal something about the scene they were portraying.

In the grand tradition of painting the emphasis was never on landscape or an historical event, which were present only as a background for man, but on man himself. Fromentin argues that the decline in painting began precisely when man's principal attention became focused on the anecdote or story and the idea arose that a painting's purpose was to present the historical subject or setting. When man's attention turned to the subject or the setting as the principal interest of the painting, the true nature of the art had been deflected from the plastic representation of Beauty to a kind of narrative genre pictorially depicted:

Qu'est-ce que le *sujet*, sinon l'anecdote introduite dans l'art, le fait au lieu de l'idée plastique, le récit quand il y a récit, la scène, l'exactitude du costume, la vraisemblance de l'effet, en un mot la vérité, soit historique, soit pittoresque? Tout se déduit et tout s'enchaîne. La logique apportée dans le *sujet* conduit tout droit à la couleur locale, c'est-à-dire à une impasse, car, arrivé là, l'art n'a plus qu'à s'arrêter; il est fini.[6]

In its vastness Nature contains the reflection of Beauty as well as the purpose and meaning of existence. As the shaper of substance Nature has the *initiative du beau* ("initiative of beauty"), yet man, too, plays a large part, for he has been granted the power through art to reveal the beautiful in nature. Thus Realism is not art but the death of art. When art is reduced to the unselective reproduction of the raw forms of nature, it is no longer art at all:

Le peintre qui bravement prendra le parti de se montrer véridique à tout prix rapportera de ses voyages quelque chose de tellement inédit, de si difficile à déterminer, que, le dictionnaire *artistique* n'ayant pas de terme approprié à des œuvres de caractère si imprévu, j'appellerai cet ordre de sujets des *documents*.[7]

By definition art implies a transformation of matter into another form and medium. Otherwise one has merely a group of "documents" which might themselves serve as a basis for art.

Fromentin did not accept the Romantic notion that poetic creativity is marked by the creation of something new. The Romantic aesthetic shifted the Neoclassical accent on form to an emphasis on the poet's originality, his ability to invent what had never been experienced before. In the Neoclassical aesthetic the artist's originality has nothing to do with his choice of subject matter. His originality lies in his ability to give whatever subject he chooses perfect form. In Fromentin's perspective the world was not an ever changing reality in which each new experience or sight represented the matter for another work of art. Essentially the world was full of many different shapes which merely repeated the simple truths in different forms:

Le monde extérieur est comme un dictionnaire; c'est un livre rempli de répétitions et de synonymes: beaucoup de mots équivalents pour la même idée. Les idées sont simples, les formes multiples; c'est à nous de choisir et de résumer.[8]

The myriad of forms repeated to infinity are important for the significant truths and the image of beauty reflected in them.

At the beginning of part three of *Une Année*, Fromentin describes the spectacular Negro celebration known as the *Fête des fèves*. He is dazzled by the costumes, the color, and movement. It is the kind of experience which most travelers and artists would have considered the highlight of their trip. It was an opportunity to see something entirely new, something which very few Europeans could have experienced. The Romantic artist would have delighted in the novelty of the scene and would have described it in all its detail. Fromentin's response to the spectacle is quite different:

C'était fort beau, et dans cette alliance inattendue du costume et de la statuaire, de la forme pure et de la fantaisie barbare, il y avait un exemple de goût détestable à suivre, mais éblouissant. Au reste, ne parlons pas de goût dans un pareil sujet. Pour aujourd'hui, laissons les règles. Il s'agit d'un tableau sans discipline, et qui n'a presque rien de commun avec l'art. Gardons-nous bien de le discuter; voyons.[9]

Although Fromentin was attracted by what he saw, declaring it both "fort beau" and "éblouissant," he concluded that it had little in common with art. He compared it with a "tableau sans discipline" lacking any sense of taste or proportion. Without measure, proportion, harmony, balance, and good taste art was not possible.[10] One could have a colorful spectacle, a feast for the eyes, but art involved form and a sense of what was beautiful.[11] Although eye-catching, the bizarre sight of movement and color had no more to do with art than the ugly cluster of flies on the child's lip,[12] a detail which Fromentin only reluctantly included in his travel account. Both incidents violated good taste and were remarkable only as extraordinary sights from among the numberless forms provided by the dictionary of life.

III   The Artist's Role

Fromentin's perspective of art is the legacy of the Ptolemaic universe where man is the center of God's creation, a microcosm of the macrocosm, the image of the universe in miniature:

. . . un art qui consistait à faire choix des choses, à les embellir, à les rectifier, qui vivait dans l'absolu plutôt que dans le relatif, apercevait la nature comme elle est, mais se plaisait à la montrer comme elle n'est pas. Tout se rapportait plus ou moins à la personne humaine, en dépendait, s'y subordonnait et se calquait sur elle . . . . Il en résultait une sorte d'universelle humanité ou d'univers humanisé, dont le corps humain, dans ses proportions idéales, était le prototype.[13]

Man is unique because he not only shares the property of matter with the rest of creation, but he is the only creature privileged to share in the divine spirit through his intellect. Since the universe was made for man's use, it is no wonder that man must be the focal point and his history and setting only important insofar as they illuminate his nature: "La nature existait vaguement autour de ce personnage absorbant."[14] Man alone can look at the enigma of chaotic matter and perceive the ordered harmony and beauty which underlies nature.

Chose admirable et accablante, la nature détaille et résume tout à la fois. Nous, nous ne pouvons tout au plus que résumer, heureux quand nous le savons faire! Les petits esprits préfèrent le détail. Les maîtres seuls sont d'intelligence avec la nature; ils l'ont tant observée, qu'à leur tour ils la font comprendre. Ils ont appris d'elle ce secret de simplicité, qui est la clef de tant de mystères.[15]

The artist is that privileged man who is graced by the ability to penetrate the surface of life, to make order out of chaos, and to communicate his vision in a form which makes the essential reality or beauty apparent to others. In a sense the artist is not a creator, in that he does not create the beauty which lies hidden within the multitude of nature's forms. Nevertheless, it is he who transforms these shapes to reveal the beauty within. In looking at a familiar scene of children playing Fromentin asks:

Sont-ce des enfants qui jouent dans le soleil? Est-ce une place au soleil dans laquelle jouent des enfants? La question n'est pas inutile, car elle détermine avant tout deux points de vue très différents. Dans le premier cas, c'est un tableau de figures où le paysage est considéré comme accessoire; dans le second, c'est un paysage où la figure humaine est subordonnée, mise au dernier plan, dans un rôle absolument sacrifié.[16]

The artist chooses what to emphasize and what details should be used. It is he who transforms raw matter into a work of art.

IV *The Importance of Memory*

A number of scholars have discussed and compared the role of memory in the works of Fromentin and Proust.[17] For both writers the memory plays a major role in their literary production. To Fromentin, who all his life pursued the absolute quality of things, the timeless and immutable, memory provided a means of fixing the essence of the self in an otherwise constantly changing reality:

La manie des dates, des catégories chez Dominique lui vient donc de sa préoccupation de retenir les moments de conscience et du souci de ne pas se perdre de vue.[18]

Memory allows one to maintain contact with one's former self, to maintain a continuity of being. Through memory and habit one can establish a continuity of being which approaches the absolute:

Se souvenir ainsi, c'est s'habituer à une prise de conscience par laquelle on saisit son unité intérieure. Ce n'est pas le passé qui remonte à travers le temps qui nous en sépare, mais l'être que l'on était dans ce passé et qui vient se fondre en la mêmeté de celui que l'on est.[19]

From his early years in Paris to the 1874 preface to his travel literature, Fromentin remains constant in the value he placed on the role of memory in the creative process. As mentioned above Fromentin did little painting while his model was before him. He sketched, took notes, and depended on his memory to recall the details of the subject and scene. Far from considering such a method of composition detrimental to the creative process, he considered the period of gestation of the greatest value:

Elle me rendit toute sorte de services. Surtout, elle me contraignit à chercher la vérité en dehors de l'exactitude et la ressemblance en dehors de la copie conforme.[20]

In *Une Année dans le Sahel* Fromentin points out how difficult it was to produce a work of art. The artist faces many difficulties, not the least being the pressure to exhibit the "documents" which the artist brings back from his travels. Public interest in ethnography is so great and the adulation of the "documents" so extensive that the temptation is hard to resist:

Il y a un plaisir irrésistible à dire d'un pays que peu de gens ont visité: je l'ai vu. . . . Il faut être plus modeste encore,—et cette modestie-là devient un principe d'art,—pour résumer tant de notes précieuses dans un tableau, pour sacrifier la propre satisfaction de ses souvenirs à la vague recherche d'un but général et incertain. Disons le mot, il faut une véritable abnégation de soi-même pour cacher ses études et n'en manifester que le résultat.[21]

In Fromentin's eyes the Realist passes off his "études" as works of art. The true artist recasts his materials into works of art. For Fromentin the memory is the "outil créateur" which strips away unnecessary and insignificant details. With the passage of time the mind's eye condenses the focus to the essential nature and beauty of the tableau. Fromentin wrote on 17 November 1844:

Les souvenirs sont d'une lucidité merveilleuse; ils s'enchaînent, se développent, se multiplient ou se résument avec un ordre parfait. Les endroits obscurs de la vie s'éclairent, les mystères du coeur se découvrent, tant il fait grand jour au dedans de nous-même . . . enfin les perspectives indéfinies du temps s'entr'ouvrant du même coup . . . l'inconnu lui-même se révèle et se laisse entrevoir; les jugements sur le passé sont rigoureux, les prévisions presque infaillibles.[22]

In a letter of 16 August 1846 Fromentin signals the importance of memory to the artistic form of his work:

En passant par le souvenir, la vérité devient un poème, le paysage un tableau. Si grande et si belle que soit la réalité, tu verras que le souvenir finit encore par la dépasser et réussit à l'embellir. Je suis bien sûr que tout ce que j'ai vu il y a trois mois reste maintenant au-dessous de l'image transfigurée que j'en ai gardée . . . . [23]

In all of Fromentin's work, except *Maîtres d'autrefois*, memory played an essential role. It shaped his novel from the experiences of his youth, transformed his journeys to North Africa into sketches and paintings, and reworked his impressions of Algeria into his two travel books.

CHAPTER 3

The Painter

I The Romantic Years

WHEN Fromentin turned toward painting in the early 1840s, he entered an artistic world in the process of great change. The attack against traditional French thought was as apparent in the theory and practice of art as it was in philosophy, politics, literature, and religion. By the 1840s the battle lines were shifting away from the issues which had dominated the early Romantic years and which had divided supporters of Ingres from those of Delacroix:

Il avait semblé que l'avenir de la peinture fût lié à la prédominance de la ligne sur la couleur ou de la beauté sur le caractère. Ces questions, sans être résolues, allaient passer au second plan et c'est un autre problème, également éternel, celui des rapports légitimes entre l'art et la société, qui allait susciter les enthousiasmes et les colères.[1]

The question of color versus line was only one of many issues which Romanticism spawned in its rebellion against the Classical tradition, symbolized in the early nineteenth century by the school of David. By the early 1840s the accepted hierarchy of subject matter, which traditionally placed canvases of great historical interest in the highest category and landscape and genre toward the bottom, had been brought into serious question. Just as poets still revered the epic poem and dreamed of crowning a career with such a masterwork, many painters still held the large historical canvas in great esteem, but genre and landscape had risen considerably and were no longer automatically relegated to an inferior position.[2]

Interest in the Near East had been high in French art and literature for some time. Prior to the 1830s the Orient had served both writers and painters who wished to exercise their fantasy or imagination on an exotic subject. Because of the underlying classic notion that man's nature is basically constant wherever he may live in the world, there was little motivation to travel to the site of a scene one hoped to paint. The opening of the Near East to French travel, however, coincided with an increasing interest among Romantic writers and artists who believed that one's work should be provided with an authentic setting and values. Delacroix, Decamps, and Marilhat all traveled to parts of North Africa and the Near East and all represented to the generation prior to 1840 a move toward greater accuracy in painting the Orient. In truth interest in the depiction of North Africa in a realistic sense was only slight. Delacroix never revisited Morocco, and yet he continued to produce paintings set in North Africa. Not only did he consider his memory sufficient, but in his aesthetic perspective he placed greater emphasis on his vision of the area than on the object itself.

In the 1840s the movement toward Realism drew many artists away from the classic notion of nature in which man plays the supreme role, as well as from the Romantic use of imagination in the transformation of subject matter. Because of the emphasis on reality itself, many saw the function of art as the reproduction of that reality in an objective sense. Those interested in contemporary social and economic problems realized that art could play a major role in bringing about the change which they hoped to make in society. Humanitarians and utopian philosophers enlisted the support of artists to communicate the political, social, economic, and philosophical ideas which they had espoused. It was common to portray, in realistic terms, humble, contemporary scenes which conveyed the desired social message in symbolic form or by suggestion. But the encouragement given by such critics as Jules Castagnary to realistic paintings which, as one would say today, manifested a social awareness was not the only support for Realism in art. There were others, whom Joseph Sloane calls objective naturalists, who had no political goal but attempted to place on canvas exactly what they found in reality, a kind of purist's approach with the emphasis on mimetic form. When Fromentin first became interested in painting as a career, Gustave Courbet, who was to become the foremost Realist, had not yet burst on the scene. Nonetheless, the trend toward Realism in art was unmistakable.

As mentioned in chapter 1, Fromentin's father grudgingly permitted him to study painting and placed him for a short time in the studio of Rémond, often treated by critics as a completely untalented painter of the much scorned academic school of painting. The impression is left that Fromentin's father was a narrow bourgeois who knew nothing about real art and chose Rémond only because of his own rigidly conservative tastes. The perspective would have been quite different in Fromentin's time. Léon Rosenthal points out that, despite the realistic trend in landscape painting under the Constitutional Monarchy, the Ecole Impériale still ruled supreme in 1830 and that Bertin, Bidauld, and Rémond all remained active for more than a decade after the monarchy's inception. In fact, Neoclassic landscape enjoyed great success until 1840 and only gradually declined as the brief fad for Neoclassical art subsided. Moreover, if one considers the theories of landscape painting which they espoused, one realizes that Fromentin himself must have found their principles quite acceptable. Although they painted landscapes, they emphasized that nature was not the primary subject of their work. In all art man must be preeminent, they argued, and the landscape was perceived only as a setting. The artist was a seeker and creator of beauty. Out of the chaos of nature he made order. By his artistic perception and craft, he reconstructed and idealized nature to bring out the harmony and order which lay beneath the enigma of surface reality. Their known distaste for what was imprecise and vague, their dislike of sudden change and spring, and their love of permanence and autumn are all sentiments which Fromentin shared and which came to be hallmarks of his work.[3]

Yet he remained with Rémond only briefly. When he chose to work with Cabat, he was associating himself with an artist known at the time, along with Rousseau, Dupré, and Diaz, as a leader among landscape painters in directing art toward a realistic presentation of the genre. In spite of all the points of agreement between Fromentin and the academic school, he felt that too much emphasis was placed on imitation of the masters and not enough interest in the observation of reality. This was, of course, not a necessity to the Neoclassical artist since the landscape used as background was frequently an idealized Greece or Rome. In principle Fromentin undoubtedly agreed that one did not need to paint from a model. That Fromentin should even use a contemporary landscape and seek to become familiar with it was a sign of the times. In his own aesthetic perspective and practice landscape played only a secondary role. However, he took detailed notes concerning the landscapes that he would paint, even though he felt no need to paint with the model before him. Rather, he preferred composition from memory and even saw it as an important element in the creation of art. The notes served to characterize the place, the customs, or the individual so that his memory might perceive the essential traits in the details of the general impression.

II *Beginnings of Success*

As mentioned previously, Fromentin made three journeys to North Africa, one for six weeks in 1846, another for eight months in 1847–48, and a third for nearly a year in 1852–53. Each trip marks an important stage in Fromentin's development as a painter. The first trip persuades him that he has a special affinity for North Africa and that much remained to be said pictorially about the region, despite the numerous paintings that had already been made.

After his first trip he had three paintings accepted for exhibition at the Salon of 1847, one portraying a farm in the vicinity of La Rochelle, the other two scenes inspired by his trip to North Africa. Not much attention was paid to these paintings, heavily influenced by the style of painting he had learned in Cabat's studio. In 1888 Charles Bigot wrote that "Une Ferme aux environs de la Rochelle" was so crude that any student from the Ecole des Beaux Arts could do better and that no jury of his day would have accepted the work.[4] Contrarily, the two North African canvases showed the promise of the future and encouraged Fromentin, who embarked on his second and longer trip to the African continent for more inspiration. Fromentin did not enter the Salon of 1848, but he had five paintings accepted for the 1849 exhibition. On this occasion his work received good attention for a relative newcomer and his second-place medal and the sale of some of his work was promising. As he wrote to Lilia Beltrémieux, his position was now much more secure. His work had been mentioned favorably in a number of reviews, and he had received a second-place medal and a government subsidy for the year to come. He had been able to pay some of his debts with the sale of his paintings and the medal assured his place at future salons without passing the jury.[5] The following year Fromentin exhibited eleven paintings at the salon and had considerable success with the critics and the public. Even though his paintings did not bring him the income they should have, he was successful enough to venture into marriage in 1851 and to make his final journey to Algeria in 1852–53.

Louis Gonse sees this as one of the two periods of major change in Fromentin as a painter. It is the period when he develops his own originality, strength, and style. One can see it in the numerous drawings which he made during the journey:

Ce sont des études sur nature, rapides et par conséquent de facture large, sommaire, grossoyée et même brutale, de caractère net, incisif, avec la dominante d'effet mise en saillie. Les extrémités, les mains et les pieds sont à peine indiqués, mais le mouvement en est juste, cursif, d'une éloquence dans bien des cas exquise.[6]

Although he still finds his use of the instrument awkward at times, he has learned to express with a sureness of hand exactly what he hopes to portray. He became admired for his ability to capture the nobility of the rude, warrior quality of the desert nomads. By accent and choice of detail, he discloses the inner spirit of Algeria and brings out forcefully and without exaggeration the violence in the manners of the country.

When he returned from the 1852–53 trip, Fromentin was preoccupied with the publication of his travel books. His seven entries in the 1857 Salon were very successful, the painting *Diffa, réception du soir* enjoying particular favor for its rich presentation of the scene described in *Un Eté dans le Sahara*. But the success of the 1857 Salon was exceeded by the five paintings presented at the Salon of 1859, which Louis Gonse calls the "Salon Roi" of Fromentin's career. Fromentin won a first-class medal at this Salon and was awarded the cross of the Legion of Honor. But for Gonse it represents the apex of Fromentin's first style of painting, the culmination of the personal style which he began to achieve during his last visit to Algeria. In *Audience chez un Khalifat dans le Sahara* Fromentin seizes the rugged, primitive vigor of the Arab chieftains, the drama of the meeting in majestically stark surroundings, highlighted by sharply contrasting colors. Henry Houssaye considered the *Audience* to be the first work to show the serious personality of the artist, brilliant in its use of light and in the warmth of its colors. Houssaye praised Fromentin for his firm use of the brush and for the solid texture of his paints, two areas where he had been criticized previously.[7]

Rue à El-Aghouat is one of Fromentin's most striking paintings. The portrayal of the dazzling light of the desert without any relief from cloud or foliage was a commonplace of Orientalist paintings. Fromentin realized that the effect of the light was not the same as it was presented in the work of his predecessors and sought to discover the means of conveying the impression it made on the inhabitant. He noticed in particular that the light did not seem so white or bright as it was painted, but that it was diffuse. He perceived that the most noticeable difference in the desert sunlight occurred when one looked into the shadows cast by buildings. Because of the brilliance of the sun, the shadows seemed nearly opaque by contrast. Yet when one adjusted to them or removed the effect of the light, he realized that what had seemed like darkness was really broad daylight. In *Rue à El-Aghouat* the swath of sunlight which runs up the street diagonally through the center of the painting has the effect of nearly hiding from view the people lying in the shade of the buildings in the lower left hand side of the painting. Only the lighter color of their garments brings them to view. The remainder of the painting, rendered in various shades of gray, helps set off the blazing, sunlit street, virtually motionless and silent, the only sign of consciousness being the woman about to enter a building across from the reclining figures, a dog in the distance, and a few birds hovering in the sky.

III *Toward a New Style*

The slate-gray colors of the noted Realist painter Corot became a trademark of Fromentin's style after 1859. Louis Gonse considered *Lisière d'oasis pendant le sirocco* (sometimes called *Le Simoun*), another of the 1859 offerings, Fromentin's finest painting, one which formed a link between his first manner and the style he would develop in the 1860s. The painting received nearly universal praise for its poetic subject, the realistic portrayal of the storm, and the quality of the technique employed. One is reminded of the description in *Un Eté*, of the sense of remoteness, silence, and dryness on the edge of the desert. The ominous low clouds lean heavily toward the corner of the painting as if blown with great force. The atmosphere is tinted by various shades of gray as Fromentin seeks to portray the appearance of the sand-filled air blown by the violent winds of the storm. Many have joined Gautier in praise of Fromentin's use of shades and halftones in creating the appearance of just the right atmospheric conditions. It is this use of grays and the lack of sharp contrast which have caused Gonse and others to see the painting as a transition toward the technique Fromentin adopted after 1861.

Throughout the 1860s Fromentin regularly contributed to the Salons. In 1861 he exhibited six paintings and in 1863 he presented *Chasse au faucon en Algérie (La Curée)* and *Fauconnier arabe*, two of his best-known works. Louis Gonse notes a number of shifts in Fromentin's work in addition to his becoming a harmonist rather than a colorist. There is a marked shift in his scenes from the dry Sahara to the more fertile Sahel with its softer colors. As a consequence one sees more foliage and the use of shades of green, blue, and gray.

Prominent in much of Fromentin's work is the horse, proud, fierce, spirited, and elegantly aristocratic. It is clear from the many hunting scenes and *fantasias* which Fromentin drew and painted that he was fascinated by the Arab on horseback. In his travel accounts he objected to those who used the Orient to clothe the Bible in local color. In making an assessment of the Arab character, Fromentin came to the conclusion that he was two figures: on foot he was the prosaic, biblical figure;[8] on horseback he became the fierce, epic warrior, independent and heroic. Fromentin saw in man and the horse " . . . les deux créatures les plus intelligentes et les plus achevées par la forme que Dieu ait faites."[9] Separate them, however, and both were reduced to a lower quotient. Philosophically man represented the intellect and the will, the horse strength and quickness. Together they formed one perfect creature:

> . . . mêlez l'homme au cheval, donnez au torse l'initiative et la volonté, donnez au reste du corps les attributs combinés de la promptitude et de la vigueur, et vous avez un être souverainement fort, pensant et agissant, courageux et rapide, libre et soumis.[10]

Fromentin saw in this ideal the union of spirit and matter, the Greek ideal of joining the mind and body.

His 1868 painting *Centaures et Centauresses s'exerçant au tir de l'arc* was criticized heavily because it was a departure from Fromentin's expected North African setting. In future offerings, such as the Venice paintings offered in 1872 and the Egyptian paintings in 1876, Fromentin attempted to expand from the narrowly North African settings with which he was associated. Maxime Du Camp wrote that he lamented his stereotype as a painter of North African scenes and disliked beginning the same old subjects over and over again for potential buyers.[11] Perhaps the unfortunate thing about Fromentin's career as a painter is that he came to be seen as a type of artist he himself detested. He always insisted that his interest in North Africa was not merely realistic or for purposes of depicting curious details of life unseen by Europeans. He was primarily interested in man; the history and landscape of the area he saw only as background and setting. He eliminated details which did not add to or seemed to get in the way of the essential trait he was trying to depict. His hostility to the anecdote and genre painting as the source of the decline in great painting surely indicates that he aspired to something greater himself.

Louis Gonse was correct in saying that Fromentin " . . . eût voulu être un peintre d'histoire . . . ," that he " . . . rêva toujours de passer de la vie réelle et des anecdotes à la vie idéale et à l'épopée."[12] His refusal to sell or exhibit the numerous sketches and incomplete studies which he had made until he could transform them into works of art shows his intention. If not in a single painting, at least in the ensemble of his work he saw the matter for a work of epic proportions. Fromentin's relentless pursuit of the nature of the desert, the climate, and the Arab within his historical and geographical setting (in both his travel books and paintings) shows his unceasing attempt to define an aspect of mankind within the North African environment.

He understood his own limitations, as his comment on the *fantasia* in *Une Année* makes clear:

Ce spectacle attend son peintre. Un seul homme aujourd'hui saurait le comprendre et le traduire; lui seul aurait la fantaisie ingénieuse et la puissance, l'audace et le droit de l'essayer.[13]

One is reminded, sadly, of Fromentin's own self-assessment, written many years earlier, in a letter to Paul Bataillard. He discusses the difficulties he was having in painting the human form and giving his work a sense of life and animation. But he is even more concerned by what he perceives to be his own lack of vision as an artist:

Enfin, chose non moins grave, je vois *joli* et pas *grand*; c'est peut-être de tous mes défauts, celui qui me désole le plus, parce que c'est un défaut de nature qui ne sera jamais tout à fait corrigible.[14]

Fromentin never found the way to make his subject into historical or epic canvases. Critics are fond of pointing out weaknesses which kept him from becoming one of the foremost painters of the day. In his early years, critics say, he was too imitative and lacked the technical skills which additional study of human and animal figures might have improved; he lacked the technique of using the brush and mixing paints. Others feel that he was too intellectual, that his aesthetic perspective, which encouraged him to paint from memory, robbed the canvas of the life which vivid details can provide. Maxime Du Camp wrote that Fromentin had a good sense of composition but lacked the ability to create a unity among the parts. In his eyes the human figures always seemed added on to the vividly detailed accessories, such as saddles and arms.[15] He attributed this to Fromentin's habit of painting his figures from memory while his accessories were copied from models. Many criticized Fromentin's classicizing perspective, his tendency to cut away the realistic details.

Much of the criticism leveled at Fromentin's shortcomings stem from writers whose own aesthetic perspective was either heavily oriented toward Realism or saw in the intellectually oriented classical perspective a hindrance to the free development of one's creative impulse. This is primarily a bias of the modern era and must be seen in its historical context. Fromentin's lack of formal training seems to be a well-established fact and was probably a hindrance to his progress as a painter. And he may have been unable to see *grand*. But the reason for his not becoming one of the masters of the period cannot be attributed to his lack of training or his intellectuality. Of the more than 2,000 active painters in the 1840s and 1850s, Fromentin is one of the very few whose work is still mentioned in standard works on nineteenth-century French painting. One need not apologize for not being Ingres, Delacroix, Courbet, or Manet and it is impossible to say why Courbet and not Corot. One can distinguish the work of the masters from the work of those who are merely great, but one can scarcely know what created the one and not the other. Fromentin was a painter of quality, and when one adds his accomplishments as a novelist and art critic he stands out among the creative minds of the nineteenth century.

CHAPTER 4

Travel Literature

I *Publication and Content of* Un Eté *and* Une Année

AFTER his brief six-week trip in 1846 persuaded him that he could make a significant contribution to art within the framework of the Oriental setting, Fromentin felt that he must return to Africa for a long period of time to become acquainted with the customs and people, to absorb as much of the atmosphere and visual surroundings as possible. He had reached a crossroad in his career and knew that he must persuade his father that it was time for him to move away from the imitation of other painters to develop his own conception and style by direct contact with the subject matter of what he conceived as his future canvases.[1] With considerable reluctance, Fromentin's family permitted the trip, an eight month sojourn which lasted from September 1847 to May 1848.

As Fromentin explained on numerous occasions, he did not expect to return from Africa with paintings ready to be submitted to the Salons. The eight-month period provided an opportunity for study and analysis. Because of his aesthetic ideas and artistic practices, the true work of art would be developed later from paintings done largely from memory. What he brought back from Africa were numerous sketches and drawings as well as a journal which reflected on and described what he had seen and experienced. It was the habit of maintaining a journal which would lead to the publication of his two travel books.

During his year-long stay from November 1852 to October 1853, he seriously considered publishing some of his reflections and sent materials to Armand du Mesnil prior to his return.[2] At the time he was discouraged about his artistic production and was not optimistic about his ability to create paintings of value from the material produced during the trip. Later, in the preface written for the 1874 edition, Fromentin wrote that the "insuffisance de mon métier me conseilla, comme expédient d'en chercher un autre, et que la difficulté de peindre avec le pinceau me fit essayer de la plume."[3] Taking into consideration Fromentin's modesty and the fact that his career as a painter would gain its greatest impetus from this period in North Africa, one need not imagine that he was seriously considering a shift in career. Financially he was always in need and the travel book offered some hope of remuneration. But another reason for his interest involves his aesthetic values and the relationship he saw between painting and literature.

Many artists of the period were exploring the relationships among the arts and some believed that language, if used poetically, could evoke or create as vivid an image of a scene in the imagination as a painting itself. Théophile Gautier, one of the foremost critics and writers of the day, had begun his career as a painter and was especially interested in the transposition of the arts and the aesthetic problems involved. He was admired for his descriptive passages in his short narratives, travel books, and poetry, and for his innovative use of language and ability to create unusually striking effects. Fromentin was also interested in defining the limits of visual representation when using the brush or pen. But he did not believe that the two art forms were able to express the same thing: "Il est hors de doute que la plastique a ses lois, ses limites, ses conditions d'existence, ce qu'on appelle en un mot son domaine."[4] In fact he distinguished clearly between the two forms of perception required for each medium. Although one may recognize the subject of a painting in a given passage of *Un Eté* or *Une Année*, the written text provides a valuable dimension which the plastic art cannot represent:

Il y a des formes pour l'esprit, comme il y a des formes pour les yeux; la langue qui parle aux yeux n'est pas celle qui parle à l'esprit. Et le livre est là, pour nous répéter l'œuvre du peintre, mais pour exprimer ce qu'elle ne dit pas.[5]

It was not merely his own inability to express on canvas what he understood about North Africa, but a belief in the complementary nature of the two art forms which motivated him to publish his reflections on Algeria in literary form.

Publication of *Un Eté dans le Sahara* did not occur immediately following his return from Algeria. After a year of revisions, it finally appeared slowly in the recently established *Revue de Paris*. Because the book did not appear regularly in the journal, it did not receive much attention. However, the January 1857 publication in book form by Lévy drew warm praise from some of the most important literary critics of the period. Later that year Théophile Gautier's periodical, *l'Artiste*, published a portion of what would become *Une Année dans le Sahel* under the title *Alger, fragment d'un journal de voyage*.[6] The *Revue des Deux Mondes* was persuaded to issue the entire volume, which appeared in 1858 under the title *Une Année dans le Sahel. Journal d'un absent*. Once again Lévy produced the text in book form in 1859.

Both texts, written in epistolary format, are drawn from Fromentin's 1852–53 visit to Algeria with some reminiscences included from his earlier trip in 1847–48. When taken together, the two volumes actually cover the entire period from November 1852 to October 1853. However, *Un Eté*, although published first, really covers the period from May to August 1853, when Fromentin traveled from Blida to Laghouat and Aïn-Mahdy. In his August 29 letter to Armand du Mesnil, Fromentin outlined the contents of the volume as he imagined it then:

Il y aurait trois parties: 1. de Médéah à Laghouat; 2. Laghouat; 3. et, comme accessoire, Aïn-Mahdy.[7]

Essentially he did not revise the basic plan of the book. In the initial section he addresses letters to his correspondent from various stages along the route from Medeah to Laghouat: Boghari, Djelfa, and Ham'ra. Included at the beginning, however, is a long and interesting description of El Kantara, a reminiscence from the visit of 1847–48, and one of the most spectacular sites along the route from Philippeville to Biskra. On the way to Boghari he mentions the hill people and describes in some detail the Diffa, an elaborate dinner provided by the Caïd in honor of the travelers. At Djelfa Fromentin concentrates on the stunning silence and dazzling light which he encounters in this remote area. The letter from Laghouat describes the recently besieged town, gives a panorama from his room, traces briefly the town's history, and describes the *rue des marchands* and the desert, again with special attention given to the relationship of light and darkness, as perceived by the observer, and the difficulties of transmitting the nuances visually on canvas. At Tadjemout and Aïn Mahdy Fromentin's physical descriptions are brief. He concentrates more on the encounter with the feared tribe of the Ouled-Sidi-Scheik, which he describes in some detail, and the religious atmosphere at Aïn-Mahdy.

Une Année follows the course of the year in its entirety, except for omission of the May to August period described in *Un Eté*. Chronologically *Un Eté* would fall between parts three and four of *Une Année*, which follows a different plan of organization. In the first part Fromentin concentrates on Mustapha. He describes his house and surroundings as well as the Arab sector. But the greatest part of this section of the book focuses less on physical description of places or customs than on matters which define the character of the place and its people. He discusses Arab/French relations, tries to isolate the real feeling of the Arabs toward the French, contrasts the Moors and Arabs, and discourses on various unrelated subjects: the use of hashish, the presence of the *rossignol* ("nightingale"), the coming of winter and rain, and the inner relationship between the landscape and the Arab's character.

In part two the author is at Blida. Here he meets his close friend Vandell and begins to see Haoûa, a woman he first encountered in part one. Book three finds him back at Mustapha. A short section, it contains principally a description of the "fête des fèves" and Fromentin's reflection on the nature of this celebration and its relevance to painting and aesthetics. Part four discovers Fromentin just after his return from the terribly hot summer trip described in *Un Eté*. The September section is a long discussion of art, followed by the lengthy narration of the October hunt. Finally, at the end of October, Fromentin describes at great length the *fantasia* which ends in Haoûa's death. A brief epilogue recounts the departure of Vandell and Fromentin's return to France.

In *Un Eté* Fromentin's letters follow the itinerary of the journey, although there is only scarce reference to the daily activities associated with the trip. Very early in the book the reader realizes that Fromentin is interested basically in the human character of North Africa. In many instances the text uses a physical description of place as a point of departure for extended discussions of Arab customs and character. In *Une Année* physical description plays even a smaller role. It is clear that Fromentin attempts to give the book a dramatic unity and more human interest by adding the important characters, Vandell and Haoûa.[8] The narrative is organized loosely around his relationship with these two personages (especially his association with Vandell), though the narrative thread serves largely as a flexible frame for his observations. In addition one can see the author's attempt to add unity to the narrative by weaving a pattern of recurring motifs indirectly related to his relationship with Haoûa.

II *Travel Literature and Fromentin*

The beginning of travel literature as a literary genre is linked to French commercial interests in the Far East in the seventeenth century under the reign of Louis XIV. Various trade ventures, followed by church missionaries, soon established permanent links between France and the Far East. The commercial and political exchange which resulted attracted those who were curious about strange peoples and lands. The taste for exoticism, which became evident in eighteenth-century art and literature, was greatly aroused by the numerous travel accounts which entertained the readers of the period. Before 1660 there were only about ten travel narratives concerning India, several on China and Persia, and relatively few on the Near East. After 1660 and the formation of commercial, political, and religious ties, there is a marked increase in the number of travel books being published. One can cite at least forty to fifty in the last third of the seventeenth century and numerous accounts appeared until 1746, when the twenty-volume *Histoire générale des voyages* was introduced.

With Napoleon's campaign, interest in the Near East grew and French intervention in the political affairs of North Africa spurred interest in the area among businessmen as well as among artists and writers. A number of famous travel books were written by the best known Romantic writers. Chateaubriand, Lamartine, Hugo, Nerval, and Gautier all wrote travel books which were widely read for the bizarre and fascinating customs, religious beliefs, and sites which the writers described. The Romantic fondness for local color found a fertile field of cultivation in the Near East, but the fascination for the exotic and the imaginative was served as well. Some of the Romantic painters, such as Ziem, Marilhat, and Delacroix, became interested in the Near East and attempted to capture the striking differences between North Africa and Europe in terms of its physical surroundings, costume, and customs.

III *The Artistic Perspective of Fromentin's Texts*

Fromentin's interest in North Africa developed at a time when few Frenchmen had visited the area. He was the first painter to reach some of the towns he visited when he traveled south. Thus, one must realize that there was a charm in his work which cannot be appreciated today and, in fact, was largely lost even by the time he

wrote the preface to his 1874 edition. He mentions himself that North
Africa had been so often visited and written about since that only the
author could wish to see a reprinting of these travel books. While
there is much truth in Fromentin's assessment, especially if read
today, the far more engaging question is why Fromentin's travel
books should be of such durable interest when most works of this
nature quickly became outdated. The answer lies in the peculiar
nature of Fromentin's books and in his aesthetic values.

Fromentin's travel books differ in substance and intent from the
usual format of such literature. The painter adopted an epistolary
form, as if he were writing letters to a friend (Armand du Mesnil) from
various points on his journey or from the places where he stayed (such
as Mustapha and Blida) for long periods of time. The letters are
arranged in chronological order and are dated, some precisely, some
with an indication as to the month. However, very little is done to
give the letters the feeling of real correspondence, in that only rarely
does the author recall his correspondent to the reader's mind and
many of the letters far exceed the length imaginable for correspondence. Moreover, they are not filled with the daily events which
one might expect in a spontaneous exchange of letters written day by
day as the events occur. Thus there is no real effort to make the letters
seem authentic. But it is not just that the "letters" were composed
much later, it is that Fromentin's idea of what is significant and
interesting is different. Usually authors record their own experiences, especially those which play a significant role in the itinerary.
Yet Fromentin often omits important and potentially exciting portions of his trip.

During his second trip in 1847–48, Fromentin and Salzmann decided to try to escape the winter and its incessant rain. They jour-
neyed to the coast and boarded a ship to Philippeville, a crossing
which they expected to be uneventful. As it turned out the passage
was dangerous and exciting. Frequently such an experience forms
the centerpiece of a travel book otherwise filled with the usual
description of the author's surroundings and daily encounters.
Fromentin nowhere mentions the voyage to Philippeville, although
he inserts the description of El Kantara from the same trip into the
book.

As Pierre Martino[9] points out in his comparison of Fromentin's
final text with the notes of the journal from which it was drawn, the
author carefully removed numerous *je's* and *moi's* from the text to
lend it a more impersonal tone. Fromentin did not wish the book to

be a series of impressions which emphasized the vision of the author or the personal element of the author's own experience. He disliked the emotional, confessional tone often associated with personal diaries and journals from the Romantic period. Yet neither did he seek to make the text impersonal in the same sense that Gautier intended in his work. For Gautier the beauty of the tableau was what mattered—its proportion, color, and harmony. To Fromentin the emphasis on *paysage* or *anecdote*[10] for its own sake represented one of the primary reasons for the decline of French painting in the modern period. He believed that great painting must always focus on man. The setting or narrative of the painting must remain subordinate to the human interest of the painting. As a result Fromentin never really focused his attention on the countryside for its own sake nor did he place great emphasis on his own activities or even those of the region. Each setting, encounter, meditation, or discourse which he includes in the text is important because it reveals something essential about North Africa, the people, or art. Furthermore, because Fromentin gave the journal a complementary role, he sought to capture aspects of North Africa which could not be produced in plastic form.[11]

IV *Some Characteristics of* Un Eté *and* Une Année

For Fromentin North Africa was a country of extremes. In the stark grandeur of its landscape and the epic nature of its people, he saw violently clashing elemental forces. In order to appreciate the essential personality of the region, one had to understand the antithetical drives which made up its character. The violence of the contrast had the effect of heightening the difference between opposites, thereby creating an illusion which one must penetrate to see the reality. Because the light from the sun was so brilliant, the shadows cast by the buildings in the narrow passageways looked opaque at first glance and then took on the appearance of a veiled clarity as one's eyes adjusted:

Cette ombre des pays de lumière, tu la connais. Elle est inexprimable; c'est quelque chose d'obscur et de transparent, de limpide et de coloré; on dirait une eau profonde. Elle paraît noire, et, quand l'oeil y plonge, on est tout surpris d'y voir clair. Supprimez le soleil, et cette ombre elle-même deviendra du jour. Les figures y flottent dans je ne sais quelle blonde atmosphère qui fait évanouir les contours.[12]

Throughout *Un Eté* he chooses landscapes, customs, and events which reveal the antithetical nature of the country and people.

In the opening chapter he was about to begin a journey south when a violent rainstorm delayed their start. Fromentin uses the opportunity to reminisce about the trip he had made from Philippeville to Biskra in 1847–48. Just as before he wishes to escape the incessant rain of the winter season by travelling to more southerly areas not reached by the rain. The previous trip was a perfect example of the contrast afforded by the gully-washing rains which hammer the Tell and the unending summer heat of the Sahara, which turns swollen, raging ravines into trickling streams or dry gulches. The centerpiece of the chapter is his description of El Kantara, the bridge at the mountain range which divides the region covered by somber clouds and filled with blowing rain from the sundrenched plains and blue sky just beyond:

El–Kantara—le pont—garde le défilé et pour ainsi dire l'unique porte par où l'on puisse, du Tell, pénétrer dans le Sahara. Ce passage est une déchirure étroite, qu'on dirait faite de main d'homme, dans une énorme muraille de rochers de trois ou quatre cents pieds d'élévation. Le pont, de construction romaine, est jeté en travers de la coupure. Le pont franchi, et après avoir fait cent pas dans le défilé, vous tombez, par une pente rapide, sur un charmant village, arrosé par un profond cours d'eau et perdu dans une forêt de vingt-cinq mille palmiers. Vous êtes dans le Sahara.[13]

The tableau of El-Kantara allows Fromentin to portray the two seasons and the two regions which comprised for him the character of North Africa:

Aussi, est-ce une croyance établie chez les Arabes que la montagne arrête à son sommet tous les nuages du Tell; que la pluie vient y mourir, et que l'hiver ne dépasse pas ce pont merveilleux, qui sépare ainsi deux saisons, l'hiver et l'été; deux pays, le Tell et le Sahara; et ils en donnent pour preuve que, d'un côté, la montagne est noire et couleur de pluie, et de l'autre, rose et couleur de beau temps.[14]

At the same time the painter describes the oasis, the forest of palms surrounding the city, which contrasts so sharply with the desert beyond. By summer's end Fromentin lives in awe of the desert's dryness and the desperate thirst which even a relatively protected traveler can experience. By contrast, the oasis, with its water and trees, takes on the appearance of a splendidly fertile, magical paradise in the midst of desiccation. He remembers his introduction to the sunny, mysterious desert of which he grew fond and saw it as his gateway to the Orient:

Ce passage inattendu d'une saison à l'autre, l'étrangeté du lieu, la nouveauté des perspectives, tout concourut à en faire comme un lever de rideau splendide; et cette subite apparition de l'Orient par la porte d'or d' El-Kantara m'a laissé pour toujours un souvenir qui tient du merveilleux.[15]

In describing the oasis around Laghouat he emphasizes the vastness of the desert: "Elle paraît toute petite, et se presse contre les deux flancs de la ville, avec l'air de vouloir la défendre au besoin . . . ."[16] It contrasted starkly with the desert, like the small islets of civilization which were surrounded always by cemeteries: ". . . elle ressemble à deux carrés de feuilles enveloppés d'un long mur, comme un parc, et dessinés crûment sur la plaine stérile."[17]

In the letter dated El-Gouëa, 24 May, Fromentin describes the Diffa, *le repas d'hospitalité* ("the meal of hospitality"), offered to them by the "caïd," Si-Djilali. This might well offer the subject for a painting and would, most assuredly, be described by any traveler who intended to write an account of his trip. It offers an opportunity to present Arab cuisine and customs in a festive, particularly authentic atmosphere. Yet Fromentin is scarcely interested in this aspect of the scene and only describes the dinner because of a sense of obligation:

La composition en est consacrée par l'usage et devient une chose d'étiquette. Pour n'avoir plus à revenir sur ces détails, voici le menu fondamental d'une *diffa* d'après le cérémonial le plus rigoureux.[18]

For two pages he describes the ingredients and how they are eaten. Then he turns to the more important element of the feast, one not readily communicated by the brush. Using the book of Daumas as his point of departure, Fromentin notes that the custom of the Diffa represents a profoundly religious act on the part of the Arab, whom he considers to be a basically antisocial human being:

. . . tu dois voir que c'est dans les moeurs arabes un acte sérieux que de manger et de donner à manger, et qu'une *diffa* est une haute leçon de savoir-vivre, de générosité, de prévenances mutuelles. Et remarque que ce n'est point en vertu de devoirs sociaux, chose absolument inconnue de ce peuple antisocial, mais en vertu d'une recommandation divine, et, pour parler comme eux, à titre d'*envoyé de Dieu*, que le voyageur est ainsi traité par son hôte. Leur politesse repose donc non sur des conventions, mais sur un principe religieux. Ils l'exercent avec le respect qu'ils ont pour tout ce qui touche aux choses saintes, et la pratiquent comme un acte de dévotion.[19]

Moreover, the significance of the act, the piety it demonstrates, becomes readily apparent when one considers that the Arab male does not serve in his home,[20] but is served. Nothing could be more astonishing than to see the proud, rugged horseman humble himself in this way:

Aussi ce n'est point une chose qui prête à rire, je l'affirme, que de voir ces hommes robustes, avec leur accoutrement de guerre et leurs amulettes au cou, remplir gravement ces petits soins de ménage qui sont en Europe la part des femmes; de voir ces larges mains, durcies par le maniement de cheval et la pratique des armes, servir à table, émincer la viande avant de vous l'offrir, vous indiquer sur le dos du mouton l'endroit le mieux cuit, tenir l'aiguière ou présenter, entre chaque service, l'essuie-mains de laine ouvrée. Ces attentions, qui dans nos usages paraîtraient puériles, ridicules peut-être, deviennent ici touchantes par le contraste qui existe entre l'homme et les menus emplois qu'il fait de sa force et de sa dignité.[21]

At Aïn-Mahdy he takes advantage of an earlier incident to emphasize further the religious character of the people. When they were set to begin the journey toward Aïn-Mahdy, the inhabitants were preparing the feasts which signalled the expected end of Ramadan with the sighting of the new moon. Just after they leave, the fasting is declared over as the new moon is allegedly seen. At Aïn-Mahdy, however, the devout inhabitants yet look for an appearance of the new moon. When told that the people of Laghouat had already begun to feast, their answer is definite:

Mais à tout cela on nous répondit que si les Beni-l'Aghouat avaient vu la lune nouvelle, c'est qu'ils y regardaient de moins près qu'ailleurs; que dans Aïn-Mahdy on était plus formaliste, et que le jeûne durait encore.[22]

Throughout the trip Fromentin is sensitive to the fact that the Arabs detest the French. Just as the French colonial presence disturbs ordinary life for the Arabs, so does his own presence require them to entertain him and make exceptions to their traditions. One had the feeling that the farther he moved from the French settlement the purer Arab life and customs would be. The religious attitude at Aïn-Mahdy reflected the town's remoteness.[23]

In both books Fromentin attempts to convey to the reader the importance of the pervasive silence on the desert. One could scarcely know the African experience without sensing how integral to the scene and its atmosphere it was. Here was an aspect of North Africa which was vital to an understanding of the area and yet could scarcely be captured on canvas. In the letter from Djelfa, 31 May, Fromentin describes the uninterrupted horizon and tries to give an idea of the grandeur by conveying the sense and texture of the silence. It is a silence so pure that he can hear the whir of birds' wings as they pass overhead. Those who live in the tumult of city life can scarcely know its benefits and charm:

Le silence est un des charmes les plus subtils de ce pays solitaire et vide. Il communique à l'âme un équilibre que tu ne connais pas, toi qui as toujours vécu dans le tumulte.[24]

One would be wrong, however, to think that silence is merely the absence of noise:

Si je puis comparer les sensations de l'oreille à celles de la vue, le silence répandu sur les grands espaces est plutôt une sorte de transparence aérienne, qui rend les perceptions plus claires, nous ouvre le monde ignoré des infiniment petits bruits, et nous révèle une étendue d'inexprimables jouissances. Je me pénètre ainsi, par tous mes sens satisfaits, du bonheur de vivre en nomade.[25]

In *Une Année* the idea that the silence of the night carries voices and memories through the tranquil air is beautifully illustrated. Fromentin is listening in the night to the dogs barking on the plain. The sounds come from near and far and he imagines that they form an unbroken chain of communication across the entire expanse of the Sahel: from town to town and farm to farm " . . . par un écho continue jusqu'au fond de la plaine."[26] The vast silence of the desert with its echoing sound is transformed poetically into the expanse of the mind and the echoing sounds become the memories which rise up from the recent and distant past. At Laghouat he describes the desert at sundown and realizes that the true desert lies to the south in an

endless expanse of sand, in its flux limitless and permanent like the
sea:

> . . . l'immobilité de cette mer solide devient alors plus frappante que jamais.
> On se demande, en le voyant commencer à ses pieds, puis s'étendre, s'en-
> foncer vers le sud, vers l'est, vers l'ouest, sans route tracée, sans inflexion,
> quel peut être ce pays silencieux revêtu d'un ton douteux qui semble la
> couleur du vide; d'où personne ne vient, où personne ne s'en va, et qui se
> termine par une raie si droite et si nette sur le ciel.[27]

What lies beyond? The names of remote places seen only on the map
but never visited. There before him in the sunlight lies the unknown:

> J'ai devant moi le commencement de cette énigme, et le spectacle est étrange
> sous ce clair soleil de midi. C'est ici que je voudrais voir le sphinx égyptien.[28]

The silent desert, teeming with delicate sounds and unknown mysteries, is a vast being as solitary as man himself. In the tumult of
civilization the mind is occupied with the activities of the day. Here
on the desert the observer can listen to the subtle sounds of life,
which echo through time and space. These sounds recall other experiences in life, thus giving the fleeting nature of life a kind of
permanence which it does not otherwise possess. It was perhaps the
relationship between the profound, mysterious desert and the solitude of the individual which made Fromentin feel such an affinity for
North Africa.

Within the two volumes there are many other kinds of material
important to an understanding of the region and its people not easily
portrayed on the canvas. Within his presentation of the difference
between the Tell and the Sahara, Fromentin discusses the etymology
of the two words to point out the close correspondence between their
meanings and the character of the areas. At times he pauses to give a
brief historical sketch, such as his discussion of the tribal warfare, the
recent events which led to the French presence in the region, and the
bloody siege of the city less than a year prior to Fromentin's own visit.
To these more contemporary matters he occasionally adds legendary
material which helps create the native atmosphere of the region. At
Aïn-Mahdy he retells the story of Tedjini, the fabled warrior and
religious leader who was besieged by Abd-el-Kader and tricked into
leaving the city. In *Une Année* Fromentin takes pleasure in recounting the story of Si Mustapha-ben-Roumi, the adopted French boy

who eventually returned to lead his native Frenchmen against his own foster father. It is a tale which characterizes both peoples in admirable terms, especially the Arab father, whose love for his adopted son transcended even his honor as a warrior.

In addition Fromentin adds reflections and personal observations of a more contemporary nature. He dwells for some time on the difference between the Moors and the Arabs, contrasting the bourgeois, merchant-oriented Moor with the rural, militarily oriented Arab. Other discussions of interest which involve a characterization of Algeria include the presence of the *rossignol*, the use of hashish, and a brief consideration of what he knew of the judicial system. These items are all things which one customarily finds within the usual travel book. They are characteristic of Fromentin in maintaining their focus on the Arab character rather than on the factual reporting of observed phenomena.

Finally, as noted above, Fromentin makes a considerable effort to give *Une Année* a unity which *Un Eté* does not have.[29] In the first section he encounters a Moorish woman named Haoûa, whom he meets later and comes to know. In part two he visits Haoûa regularly, a divorcée who, by Arab standards, lives in a most unconventional manner. The relationship is scarcely developed between Haoûa and Fromentin, the principal focus being on the mystery surrounding her and her way of life. The reader suspects, however, that this is a story which will develop during the narrative. Actually Haoûa hardly plays a role in part three and is virtually absent from the text until her appearance at the *fantasia* near the end of the book. In the final scene involving her brutal death, Fromentin is able to demonstrate forcefully an aspect of the Arab character. Because the characteristic he wishes to highlight is the passionate commitment of the Arab in matters involving his honor, the background of the story, the dramatic scenario of the *fantasia*, and the parallel to his warlike nature are all necessary for a vivid, memorable presentation. Had he introduced her only at the conclusion, much of the reader's personal involvement would have been lost, thereby reducing the emotional content of the final scene.

A second thread of unity involves the introduction of Vandell, known to the Arabs as Bou-Djaba. Vandell is a Frenchman who has become so fond of North Africa that he never intends to return to his native land. He lives a nomadic existence among the tribes of the region and takes an interest in the geological features of the area.

Fromentin and he become close friends and spend much time together. The author introduces him in part two and closes the book with their separation in the final scene. Although it is obvious that the writer is fond of Vandell, his presence is felt more as a companion and type of colonial who characterizes the hold which North Africa can come to have on a man who feels a great affinity for the desert and the nomadic existence. Fromentin's own attachment stopped short of such a commitment, but the call was there. In chapter 3 Vandell's drawing of the geological features which fascinated him serve as the basis for Fromentin's most extensive discourse on the nature of art. In a sense Vandell is the nomadic pragmatist whose attachment to the soil represents only the material aspect of what fascinates Fromentin. Whereas Vandell loves to ride through the unknown expanse of the desert remaining close to the earth and becoming part of the desert itself, Fromentin's own attachment is to its spiritual essence. He loves to sit on the desert's edge meditating on its nature and significance. For all his attraction to it Fromentin remained French. In a sense the difference between Vandell and Fromentin exemplifies the painter's aesthetic perspective. It explains why Fromentin believed that being an Orientalist in no way limited the nature or scope of his artistic statement.[30]

V   *The Preface to the 1874 Edition*

In his 1874 preface Fromentin states that his travel books do not have the same objective interest they had when written nearly twenty years before. Nonetheless, they have a personal interest for Fromentin which remains undiminished:

Le seul intérêt qu'à mes yeux ils n'aient pas perdu, celui qui les rattache à ma vie présente, c'est une certaine manière de voir, de sentir et d'exprimer qui m'est personnelle et n'a pas cessé d'être mienne. Ils disent à peu près ce que j'étais, et je m'y retrouve. J'y retrouve également ce que j'ai rêvé d'être, avec des promesses qui toutes n'ont pas été tenues et des intentions dont la plupart n'ont pas eu d'effet.[31]

The statement is interesting for several reasons. Fromentin notes that his "manière de voir, de sentir et d'exprimer" had remained the same and was still valid. And he saw in these books "à peu près ce que j'étais" and "ce que j'ai rêvé d'être." In a sense the real Fromentin is present in the travel books, for one has not only his artistic perspective and the artist he was, but the artist who wished to fulfill the dreams set out in his discourses on art. The concluding statement reminds one of Dominique with its wistful, melancholy tone of partial regret. It lends credence to Fromentin's view, because it indicates how little he was inclined to exaggerate what he had been and accomplished. If what he says is true, then one has much to learn about Fromentin the artist from these texts.

Because of the statement of the Goncourts and a number of personal comments, Fromentin acquired the reputation of having an unusual memory, capable of recalling scenes and events in great detail even after long intervals. He claimed even to paint only from memory, although he was undoubtedly aided by the notes which he made.[32] In fact the notebooks provided much background information which would help to make the scene more vivid in his memory. Yet painting after the fact helped him to focus on a truth beyond the copying of exact detail. Fromentin's way of seeing was determined by his ideas on art, a subject which was examined in chapter 2. It is important to note here that this aesthetic perspective dominates all Fromentin's artistic efforts. It dictates what is important in the scenes that he records and it gives the painting or verbal description its focus and organization. This perspective kept Fromentin from espousing art for art's sake, despite his strong leanings, and yet made him reject thesis art or Realism.

On a more practical level there is much in the two books concerning Fromentin's analysis of the sunlight on the desert. Fromentin felt that the effects of the North African sun had not been rendered properly. In the 26 May letter from Boghari he reproaches himself for using the adjective *jaune* to describe what he sees:

. . . le mot d'ailleurs est brutal; il dénature un ton de toute finesse et qui n'est qu'une apparence. Exprimer l'action du soleil sur cette terre ardente en disant que cette terre est jaune, c'est enlaidir et gâter tout.[33]

In the following quotation Fromentin attempts to capture the nuances of this light:

. . . la lumière, d'une incroyable vivacité, mais diffuse, ne me cause ni étonnement ni fatigue. Elle vous baigne également, comme une seconde atmosphère, de flots impalpables. Elle enveloppe et n'aveugle pas. D'ailleurs l'éclat du ciel s'adoucit par des bleus si tendres, la couleur de ces vastes plateaux, couverts d'un petit foin déjà flétri, est si molle, l'ombre elle-même de tout ce qui fait ombre se noie de tant de reflets, que la vue n'éprouve aucune violence, et qu'il faut presque la réflexion pour comprendre à quel point cette lumière est intense.[34]

One should note that the description stresses the sensorial impact on the observer more than a plastic, visual description involving a specific site. The visual image was less important for helping Fromentin portray the effects of light than the sensations or impressions which he experienced. There is no doubt that the African sunlight is dazzling, but Fromentin feels that it is attenuated, as if the light were hazy. The effect of this impression even diminishes the sharp contrast otherwise provided by shadows. For Fromentin the challenge is to present the light as it really appears, not as the Frenchman would expect to see it. His task was rendered more difficult because this portrayal of light gave his paintings a character different from the traditional presentation of light on the desert.

Another question concerning the role of light in African landscape clashed with the classic mode of composition:

Une remarque de peintre, que je note en passant, c'est qu'à l'inverse de ce qu'on voit en Europe, ici les tableaux se composent dans l'ombre avec un centre obscur et des coins de lumière. C'est, en quelque sorte, du Rembrandt transposé; rien n'est plus mystérieux.[35]

The problem involves the initial intensity of shadows as seen in the brilliant sunlight. Thus, if objects are to be the central focus of a painting, the dominant tone at the center of the painting will be dark and the periphery will present the sunlight as a means of giving the shade its proper contrastive note. In this case Fromentin would seem to be concerned with the realistic portrayal of light, an attitude clearly in conflict with his aesthetic position. One must remember that his concern in this instance transcends any given day's experience. Just as in his famous rendering of the Sirocco both on canvas and in *Un Eté*, he hopes to capture the nature of the storm rather than describe his experience on this one occasion.

Finally, Fromentin mentions that he sees much of what he was and what he aspired to be in these books. If one looks closely there is indeed much of Fromentin the man and artist reflected in them, this despite the fact that the aspect of personal confession remains quite foreign to the texts.

It is easy to perceive the future art critic in his careful scrutiny of what he sees and in his objective discussions of these impressions and what they mean to one who would set the scene on canvas. There are a number of passages which deal with theoretical questions regarding art and many reflections concerning matters which will involve the technique of painting. Even his approach to a given scene which he intends to describe reflects the compositional features of a painter who had already conceived the scene as a canvas.

As a human being one sees Fromentin as both a compassionate and patriotic man. He recognizes that the Arabs will never accept the French presence (yet he states that the French are better masters than the Turks and that the Arabs themselves acknowledge this) and one senses that he sees no reason why they should. Even if the Frenchman is preferable to the Turk, he nonetheless restricts the autonomy of the inhabitants. Fromentin values privacy and solitude too much not to sense the inconvenience caused by the presence of the foreigner in a culture so different from France's. He perceives that his own party caused the Arab hosts to make exceptions to their religious customs to accommodate the Europeans hospitably and he is conscious that his own desire to paint what he saw and to describe the more intimate Arab existence was offensive and a violation of their privacy:

Décrire un appartement de femmes ou peindre les cérémonies du culte arabe est à mon avis plus grave qu'une fraude: c'est commettre, sous le rapport de l'art, une erreur de point de vue.[36]

Yet he never becomes disaffected from his homeland as did many who traveled to French Indo-China, although he notes with feeling that the cemeteries attest to the price that was paid. While he sympathizes with the feelings of the natives, he speaks with pride in commenting that France would now have the "grain basket" which once supplied the Roman Empire. Moreover, in describing Blida he deplores the mixed architectural styles then current in the city because of the disharmony produced. Despite his admission that Blida was beautiful prior to the war, he does not lament that the French have imposed a foreign style on the natural setting. Rather, he looks forward to the day when the entire face of Blida will become French. Currently the city resembles an Arab woman who has lost her youth and is dressing in French style. When the entire city is rebuilt in French style, harmony will be restored and the city will regain its symmetry and beauty.[37]

That Fromentin was a man of reason, cut from the classic mold, is evident in many aspects of the books. He has the sensitivity to nature and beauty which Romantics considered basic to the artistic personality. But he never allows his own feelings or impressions to dominate the text. Beauty and art always remain in the forefront, not his own personality. Similarly Fromentin's relationship to nature differs markedly from that of the Romantics. When he discusses a landscape, even though one can perceive his own personal sensitivity to it, Fromentin remains objective. He does not use nature as a reflection of his own griefs and joys. He may associate certain scenes or details with other moments and experiences, but the relationship is nearly always intellectual in nature.

That he was a man of reason is especially evident in his handling of the episode concerning Haoûa and her death. Fromentin introduces Haoûa early in *Une Année* and, although she remains more mystery than personality, the reader has a certain sympathy for her. If Haoûa's conduct offends Arab mores, it is only because she does not lead the withdrawn existence expected of Arab women. Within the framework of the conflict between Haoûa and society is the relationship of Haoûa to her former Arab husband. His attitude toward her reflects the hostility of the traditional values. What is interesting is Fromentin's reaction to the events occurring during the *fantasia*. As author he comments little on the Arab feelings toward the husband after the murder. It is true that he is pursued and virtually expelled from the region. But there is no great expression of outrage. Fromentin himself watches passively as Haoûa is killed and the husband escapes. He never once complains of the injustice of the murder or indicates any effort on his part to bring the criminal to justice. Fromentin's response is not anger but resignation. His reaction is that of the person who respects the customs of another even when deeply offended. As he gazes on the dying Haoûa, he feels great grief and pity for her. There is a recognition that, as outrageous as it may seem to one with European values, a kind of order has been restored.

In some ways more can be learned about Fromentin from a study of his two travel books than from any of his other works. In them one finds the painter, the art critic who loved to discuss theory, the prose stylist, the master of description, and much of the man himself.

CHAPTER 5

Maîtres d'autrefois

I Composition of the Book

THE director of the *Revue des Deux Mondes*, François Buloz, suggested to Fromentin in 1862 that he venture into the realm of art criticism. That Buloz thought of inviting Fromentin to make such a contribution to his journal is not strange. Fromentin was both a well-known painter and writer respected for his precise use of language and literary style. In both his travel literature and in his novel, critics had praised Fromentin's literary gifts and his analytical and descriptive powers. Fromentin's work also reflected considerable thought about aesthetic values and serious consideration of the more practical aspects of painting. Moreover, Fromentin was a brilliant conversationalist, frequently impressing his friends by his discussions of art.

Fromentin did not respond to Buloz's challenge for thirteen years, although his unfinished project, *Programme de critique*, indicates that he had thought about such a contribution in the decade prior to his sudden departure for Belgium in July 1875.[1] Pierre Moisy[2] believes that Fromentin's decision to write *Maîtres d'autrefois* was ultimately motivated by the dissatisfaction he felt with his career as a painter. By the 1870s he felt trapped as an Orientalist and realized that his attempts to present canvases on other than Oriental subjects had been unsuccessful. Yet because of his financial dependence, he was forced to continue to produce work in the Oriental mode. In addition du Mesnil was encouraging him to make the trip and undertake the study.

On 5 July 1875 Fromentin left for Brussels on what would be a twenty-six-day visit to Belgium and the Netherlands. During his whirlwind tour of museums and churches, Fromentin maintained an active correspondence with his wife and friends, had something of a social life, read a little on the history of art, and managed to absorb enough of what he saw to produce a dense volume of criticism. He visited Brussels, Malines, Antwerp, The Hague, Amsterdam, Haarlem, Ghent, and Bruges before returning to Paris on 30 July. Ordinarily it was difficult for Fromentin to write, but this book fairly flowed from his pen. By mid-October he had nearly finished. He went to Paris in November and by December had completed the volume, which appeared in the *Revue des Deux Mondes* between 1 January and 15 March 1876.

II   *Nature of the Text*

In the brief preface to the text, Fromentin explains his purpose in making such a study:

Ce serait comme une sorte de conversation sur la peinture, où les peintres reconnaîtraient leurs habitudes, où les gens du monde apprendraient à mieux connaître les peintres et la peinture.[3]

Fromentin hopes to improve the understanding of art lovers by helping them learn to distinguish the good from the mediocre. By making a detailed critique of certain paintings, he demonstrates how one should approach a work and what to look for in terms of composition and technique. And because of the careful consideration of technical matters regarding a few paintings and a number of passages which discuss aesthetic questions, there is much to interest the professional painter as well.

One might ask why Fromentin chose the seventeenth-century painters from Belgium and Holland for such a study. The answer involves several factors. The Dutch painters were well known in France. By 1830 the Louvre had representative works of all the major figures except Vermeer and there were a number of large private collections with which some were acquainted.[4] By the 1820s the Flemish and Dutch artists were universally admired in France for their landscapes. Interest in Italianate landscape waned and taste for the simple Dutch scenes spread. In the 1840s the quiet bourgeois genre paintings came into vogue and in the 1850s and 1860s Taine, Thoré-Burger, and Blanc all focused critical attention on the period.

In the late 1850s, however, the influence of Flemish and Dutch painters had begun to decrease among Realists and those who would be known later as Impressionists. As long as the distinction had been maintained between the open-air sketch and the finished composition of the studio, even early Realists had turned to the masters to see how they finished their landscapes. Mid-century Realist painters, such as Courbet and Daubigny, though revealing an occasional influence, turned more and more toward nature. Fromentin was clearly disturbed by the drift away from those elements of Classical art which he espoused and considered absolutely necessary to good painting. Some of the methods and practices of the modern school seemed to him no more than the untutored painter groping for a way. It struck him as ridiculous when the problems they were struggling to overcome had been solved by past masters. Thus, as he explains in discussing the title of the book, he hopes that the work will serve an instructive purpose: "J'intitule ces pages les *Maîtres d'autrefois*, comme je dirais des *maîtres* sévères ou familiers de notre langue française . . . ."[5] Fromentin found it deplorable that schools still taught students how to write French prose by studying masters such as Pascal and Bossuet, but that no one was counseling painters that they should study similar masters to learn something about their own craft. One of Fromentin's primary purposes in studying the lowland masters, then, was didactic. He hoped that his work would serve as a corrective to what he considered the aberrations and weaknesses of contemporary art. Because of Fromentin's restraint and discretion, he was averse to criticizing contemporary painters by name. Frequently, however, he turns aside to focus on the work of the moderns and, when one inspects the study closely, it is clear that his didactic purpose had much to do with the selection and organization of materials in the book.

Many have noted that *Maîtres d'autrefois* resembles in many ways Fromentin's earlier ventures into literature. As Meyer Schapiro observes, it recalls ". . . the Salon review, the travel book, the critical essay and the private journal."[6] The general organization follows the itinerary of Fromentin's journey and the text is conversational in tone, not unlike the impression given by the letter format used in the travel books. The commentary is focused on the paintings being viewed, much like a Salon review, Fromentin choosing only a certain number to discuss. Mingled with the detailed analyses of specific paintings are brief historical, biographical, and aesthetic sketches intended to provide a broader framework for the author's criticism. Not infrequently the writer intrudes his personal enthusiasm or misgivings concerning the criticism he is making, much in the manner of the personal dialogue found in private journals.

Fromentin divided the book into three sections, ostensibly following his trip to Belgium, Holland, and back to Belgium before leaving for France. The sections are not of equal length nor is a set organization followed in each. The first Belgium section dwells almost entirely on Rubens, with only brief references to minor figures, a short discussion of Rubens's teachers, and a final essay on Van Dyck. In the section on Holland Rembrandt plays the principal role, but much more consideration is given to lesser figures. Separate chapters are devoted to Potter, Cuyp, Hals, and minor figures, and Fromentin spends more time discussing the history of the Dutch school. The final section on Belgium is a retrospective glance at the early Flemish masters Van Eyck and Memling.

André Romus writes that Fromentin's art criticism might be defined as ". . . une description encadrée d'un jugement général et d'un jugement conclusif."[7] Romus refers to Fromentin's evaluation of a given painting, but the description applies to his criticism in a broader sense, in that the critic placed the critique of specific works into a broader historical framework. It is debatable just how much Fromentin was influenced by Taine's work and theories of art criticism.[8] What is certain is that he shared contemporary views that a knowledge of the artist's background, intellectual development, and the history of the period were essential to an understanding of his work. Thus Fromentin's discussion of Rubens represents a kind of *explication de texte*, the central section of the text being a discussion of individual paintings preceded and followed by more general considerations related to the artist's work as a whole.

Fromentin begins his consideration of Rubens by discussing Brussels and how it has been undervalued as a place where one can study art. He points out that the city serves as a fitting preface for what one will find in the rest of Belgium and that one can see the trends of the painter in the works that are there. Before analyzing the holdings at Brussels, Fromentin discusses the training which Rubens received from his two teachers, Van Noort and Van Veen. In Brussels there are seven paintings which Fromentin comments on in general, pausing for longer narrative description and analysis of three in particular. The first painting which Fromentin analyzes at length is the *Miraculous Draft of Fishes* at Malines, a painting to which he devotes ten pages, even though he criticizes it rather severely. From Malines he moves to Antwerp, which he calls Rubens's fatherland. There he visits Notre Dame, the cathedral, and the museum. In the cathedral he finds that the two paintings *Descent from the Cross* and *Elevation on the Cross* are excellent canvases for demonstrating two different manners of Rubens. At the museum he makes a rather unfavorable review of a number of paintings, stopping finally at *The Last Communion of St. Francis of Assissi*, a work which he finds so moving that he is forced to leave the museum after seeing it. Fromentin's comment on the individual portraits in the *Communion of St. Francis* leads to his next chapter in which he discusses Rubens's ability as a painter of portraits. Finally, he visits Rubens's tomb and describes the painting of St. George, which Rubens had specifically painted for his resting place.

The last chapter in the section is devoted to Van Dyck, the noted portrait painter who moved to England and was responsible in part for English interest in the Dutch masters. Fromentin's purpose in presenting an entire chapter on Van Dyck was not motivated so much by his admiration for the painter's work as by the fact that Van Dyck's work so clearly derived from Rubens, that his influence on English painting further demonstrated the importance and greatness of the Flemish master.

The Holland section resembles the first by beginning with a discussion of a city, in this case The Hague. There the resemblance ends. The Hague is not a preface to Holland but a city which Fromentin greatly admires for its aristocratic, elegant quality, and which he considers one of the most uncharacteristic towns in Holland. The following chapter is a historical survey of Dutch painting as it was known at the time. For Fromentin and his generation Dutch art really came into its own only with its political independence and made its distinctive mark by developing the portrait. The question of politics here is vital to Fromentin's thesis. Holland is a bourgeois, Protestant region, an area preoccupied with everyday reality, virtually unaware of the soul. It is only natural that such a people should shift the focus of art from beauty to the close observation of reality. And it is fitting, comments Fromentin, that their favorite genre should be accurate, splendid portraits of themselves. To Fromentin the basic trend toward Realism as a goal in art is an aberration, even though he accepts close observation of detail and the copying of nature as fundamental practices. This he emphasizes in the next chapter in which he meditates on the fact that people have long since forgotten the monuments, men, and offices of government of the seventeenth century yet still flock to see the humble paintings left by the masters. What is ultimately more important, then, he asks, truth or beauty? Continuing the theme of art's supremacy in chapter 4, Fromentin discusses the aspects of Dutch art which he admired most. He marvels that such politically turbulent times should be so little reflected in the paintings of the period and praises the Dutch school for its concentration on pure painting (as he would have understood the term): "le fond moral de l'art hollandais, c'est l'absence totale de ce que nous appelons aujourd'hui *un sujet*."[9] Although he finds that the Dutch are totally lacking in imagination, their subjects being despairingly banal, he admires enormously their technical ability as painters. In the next four chapters Fromentin discusses the work of Potter and Cuyp individually, treats a number of minor figures in one chapter, and devotes a chapter to the influence of the Dutch landscape school on France after 1830.

Of the remaining seven chapters, nearly half of the section, six concern Rembrandt and the other, Frans Hals. For Fromentin it is a necessary but painful part of the volume. From the beginning his evaluation of Rembrandt does not accord with the unreserved praise which the master received from all quarters. Fromentin is disturbed by his lack of appreciation for Rembrandt's work. With trepidation he dares to criticize established masterpieces, such as *The Anatomy Lesson of Dr. Tulp* and *The Night Watch*, even after his friends and associates urged him for his own sake and the book's to tone down his criticism. After his lengthy critique of *The Night Watch*, Fromentin turns to other Rembrandt works which he considered far superior, especially the equally famous *Syndics*, which he discusses at length. He also had high praise for two paintings, *The Disciples on the Road to Emmaus* and *The Good Samaritan*, works which are now considered of doubtful attribution. In the final chapter Fromentin turns to Rembrandt's life and discusses characteristics which are important to an understanding of his work.

At the end of the book Fromentin returns to Belgium for a brief historical sketch which takes the reader to the fifteenth century and the two principal painters of the period, Van Eyck (ca. 1390–1441) and Van Minnelinghe (ca. 1433–1494), known to posterity as Memling. Fromentin attempts to place the two artists in an historical context, but because of the paucity of information at his disposal, he is forced to rely mainly on his critique of available canvases, principally the *Madonna with Canon Van der Paele* of Van Eyck and the *Mystic Marriage of St. Catherine*.

III   *Fromentin's Use of Antithesis*

It has been noted that Fromentin was particularly fond of using antithesis as a means of developing his thought.[10] In *Maîtres d'autrefois* it is what gives the book unity and provides Fromentin with his method of analysis. At first glance the critic seems to be perusing the museums of Belgium and Holland in the manner of a dilettante reporting on the paintings which strike his fancy. Basic to the entire study, however, is the contrast which Fromentin makes between aristocratic, Catholic Belgium and bourgeois, Protestant Holland, between imaginative transformation and external imitation, and, finally, between the two great masters Rubens and Rembrandt. But the use of antithesis is even more pervasive than its presence in the basic structure would indicate, for within each painter there is the struggle between the intellect and the imagination and even in Fromentin's syntax there is a tendency to use antithesis extensively.[11]

Fromentin begins his consideration of Rubens by a discussion of the two teachers who were responsible for his artistic education, Adam Van Noort and Otto Van Veen. As Fromentin portrays them no two men could be more different from one another in nature or in their approach to art.[12] Van Noort was the true Flemish genius, unchanged by foreign influences, rough to his students, temperamental, and original. Rubens remained in his tutelage for only four years, but the imprint was such that the young painter remained Flemish despite his training in Italy. Van Veen took Rubens and made him into a cultured man, trained him in the techniques of the craft and introduced him to Italy, the wellspring of art.

For Fromentin the greatness of Rubens lies in the reconciliation of these two sides of his character: the training of the intellect and the mysterious inner self which is bound up with one's subconscious and racial stock. Without the imprint of Van Noort, Rubens may have become an imitator of the Italian style, a man whose artistry would lack the spark of native genius. Without Van Veen he would have remained a vigorous but crude practitioner of the art of painting. One might see the potential genius in the work, but it would be spoiled by an inability to give it expression.[13]

Rubens had the training to paint well and to observe carefully. His creative imagination transformed the materials and cast the whole into another order of reality. When Fromentin criticized Rubens, it was because the work failed to achieve the glorious harmony necessary for greatness. Fromentin was very impressed by *The Miraculous Draft of Fishes*, pausing ten pages to describe its qualities and power. He admired Rubens's ability to paint the crude so crudely, to deal with the text in its own terms. But the work was too earthbound in subject matter, too demanding of a crude realism to allow it to become one of his great masterpieces. A similar consideration caused him to evaluate Rubens's work as a portrait painter rather harshly, a judgment which has scandalized Rubens specialists. Although Fromentin praised Rubens highly for the individual portraits, he was unimpressed by the famous portraits of Charles de Cordes and his wife, Jacqueline.[14] How could a painter so careful in observation, so excellent in depicting body and soul with just the right gesture or facial expression not be a brilliant portrait painter? The answer lies in the demands of the genre and the insistence by the patrons on realistic likeness. A great painter like Rubens, Fromentin felt, was too fettered by the restriction of imitation to be truly interested in the task. Hence, what he produced was more document than art, more photograph than masterpiece.

Interestingly enough Rubens frequently used models for the faces which appear in his paintings. He often painted his wives or even used self-portrait as in the Saint George painting. The use of real models might seem to place further restriction on the painter's imagination. This was not the case. The models were used as a mere convenience to serve the overall artistic conception of the painting. He was not trying to render a realistic likeness of the specific faces used. Here the reality was subordinate to art and not vice-versa. The artist was free to use what he needed to suit his artistic conception of the total work.

Fromentin's evaluation of Rembrandt has been the source of great controversy, in large part because of his harsh criticism of two of the master's best-known works, *The Anatomy Lesson of Dr. Tulp* and *The Night Watch*. For some critics Fromentin could not accept Rembrandt without denying his own aesthetic perspective and concept of the craft. They argue that there was a basic incompatibility between the two artists. This view takes the essay out of context and distorts the fact. Fromentin was a very severe critic, not only of the work of others but of his own. If one looks closely at his criticism of Rubens, whom he unquestionably admired, one will find that few works receive unreserved praise. Even in the masterpieces, such as the *Adoration of the Magi*, the *Elevation on the Cross*, and the *Descent from the Cross*, he finds some room for improvement and he often has severe criticism for more works than he praises. He unquestionably prefers Rubens to Rembrandt, however, and the extensive commentary on the major works makes his admiration clear.

In the case of Rembrandt, the same impression is not given, even though the ultimate judgment is favorable. To a certain extent the fault lies in the nature and organization of the essay. Instead of beginning with a general assessment of Rembrandt, he starts by dismissing the *Anatomy Lesson* bluntly as a work of a young man, one which shows potential but nothing more. After the essay on Hals, he returns to Rembrandt with *The Night Watch*, a painting he criticizes in great detail for poor use of color, lack of compositional unity and purpose, indifferent treatment of individual figures and clothing, poor proportion in characters, and an ill-advised attempt to cast an unreal light on a realistic scene. The vigor of Fromentin's attack, despite the unquestionable accuracy of many of his observations, coupled with his unwillingness to concede the possibility that the scene might not be so realistic as he insisted, has the effect of making the reader doubt his objectivity. The remainder of the essay does little to offset the initial impression, even though it is highly complimentary.[15] Indeed, if one turns the essay around, quite another impression is left.

Following the tradition of the time, Fromentin saw two rival natures in Rembrandt, the "exterior man" and the "romanesque genius." In his first guise Fromentin believed that he excelled all other Dutch painters except Hals. To emphasize his point he advises one to see the brilliant portraits in the Galleries Six and Van Loon. He is particularly high in praise of the *Portrait of Jan Six* in virtually every detail. He goes on to make a brief review of a number of Rembrandt paintings, praising many and declaring openly the unqualified genius of the great master. He praises at length *The Syndics* for the consummate group of portraits and then dwells on two paintings, the *Disciples on the Road to Emmaus* and *The Good Samaritan*, which he loves and for which he has great admiration. Fromentin claims that *The Night Watch* was merely an early work, that the great master had not yet harnessed the powers of his genius, and that his later work demonstrated how much he had progressed. His final evaluation is important:

. . . ce grand portraitiste est avant tout un visionnaire, que ce très exceptionnel coloriste est d'abord un peintre de lumière, que son atmosphère étrange
est l'air qui convient à ses conceptions, et qu'il y a en dehors de la nature, ou
plutôt dans les profondeurs de la nature, des choses que ce pêcheur de perles
a seul découvertes.[16]

But the praise in this statement is diminished by certain factors. The
two principal paintings which Fromentin chose to praise extensively
are no longer conceded to Rembrandt. And the critic's praise of
Rembrandt's ability as a painter of portraits is tempered by our
realization that Fromentin considered the portrait to be too much
dominated by reality. Moreover, one recalls the not very flattering
suggestion that the practical bourgeoisie and the realistic portrait are
made for one another. Finally, Fromentin's reference to Rembrandt's
use of color reminds one of his harsh attack on the master's use of light
in *The Night Watch*. There he denies that Rembrandt is a colorist,
because the tag implies one who uses color with nuance, whereas
Rembrandt floods the painting with a bright light that illuminates but
removes all sense of nuance. He objects to the term *luminariste*,
which he condemns as a neologism, and states that the adjectives,
such as *éblouissant* ("dazzling"), often used in praise of Rembrandt
are really pejorative, if one actually considers what the word implies.

Fromentin considered Rubens the greater of the two geniuses, a
seminal figure who dominated his age. Rembrandt he saw as a lonely
genius whose personal powers of creativity could have no heritage.
Nonetheless, Edmond de Goncourt was correct in his assessment of
Fromentin's criticism:

Si vous diminuez un peu mon maître Rembrandt, je vous le pardonne, parce
qu'au fond vous en parlez bien amoureusement, vous en parlez à la manière
d'un amant qui bat son adorée.[17]

Fromentin was upset by what he considered the undue reputation of
The Night Watch and he reacted strongly to demonstrate what he felt
were its weaknesses. Furthermore, the criticism of Fromentin is
always more extensive than his praise. This gives the essay a more
negative tone than Fromentin felt. The rhetorical use of antithesis
caused Fromentin to concentrate more on the disparity between the
two great painters than on Rembrandt's qualities. Even though Rembrandt's technique did not suit his aesthetic values as much as Ru-

bens's, he did recognize Rembrandt as one of the great painters of his age.

IV   *Strengths and Weaknesses*

Despite the fact that a hundred years have passed since the book's first appearance, *Maîtres d'autrefois* is still recognized as a major work of art criticism. There are a number of things, however, which readers must take into consideration. Given the change in taste, it is not strange to find Fromentin omitting some artists considered important today and emphasizing some whose work is less well regarded. Such is the case with Potter and Cuyp, minor figures today but considered worthy of separate chapters by Fromentin. Contrarily one might expect chapters on Vermeer and Brueghel, two highly regarded artists today. It should be remembered that Vermeer had just recently been rediscovered by Thoré-Burger and Brueghel represented a kind of painting which Fromentin would not have admired and would not have wished to promote.

Of course, much has been learned about the Flemish and Dutch masters since Fromentin's time and it is only natural that the historical information he had at his disposal has been revised. In general the historical sections are no longer factually reliable and the reader must also be wary of a number of interpretations which Fromentin based on incorrect facts, legends, and scanty information.[18] As mentioned above, Fromentin's study of the teachers of Rubens and the hypothetical influence they had on his development is based on doubtful traditions unsupported by documents and seen through the lens of a specific aesthetic and psychological perspective. Similar errors involve Fromentin's study of the Dutch school in chapter 2. Fromentin considered the rise of Dutch art to be a phenomenon linked with political independence. Prior to independence he saw no specifically national characteristics in the painters of the period. Today scholars have a larger number of paintings and more evidence on which to base their judgments. It is clear that the painting of the North always distinguished itself by its own style. Furthermore, because of the state of scholarship, Fromentin was led to see a cluster of painters born between 1600 and 1626, a fact which seemed to support his theory. Modern scholarship has scattered the birth dates of these painters over a broader span of time.

In a few instances Fromentin was led to some hasty generalizations because the paintings he had at his disposal were inadequate for a proper appreciation of the artist's total corpus or because the paintings he chose to discuss were later attributed to another, such as the portraits used to evaluate Rubens and the paintings no longer attributed to Rembrandt.

But if the few paintings studied led to a weakness in his historical assessments, the fact that Fromentin concentrated on a few works also represents one of the volume's major strengths. Fromentin possessed the unique skills necessary to make a close analysis of a painting in technical terms and convey the judgment in lucid prose. One of the classic examples of the text is the two-page analysis of *The Last Communion of St. Francis of Assisi*. Rarely could one find a critical review as brief and yet so complete. The text is divided into three paragraphs and follows the development of a classic explication. In the first he sets the scene of the painting, describes the costume and colors of the figures, outlines the painting's composition, points out the effect of contrast established by the simple elements and their colors, and then steps back to assess the overall, three-part composition of form and color.

Having given an excellent visual conception of the picture in form and color, Fromentin focuses on the drama of the painting within the austerity of the scene. While everything in his body and in those about him gives evidence of death, the life and urgent drama of the scene are brought out by the vivid look in the saint's eye, witness of the mind's lucidity and the religious fervor of the moment.

In the final paragraph Fromentin turns his eye to the entourage to describe the different forms of grief etched in the facial expressions and gestures of the witnesses. The starkness of their grief joined with the image of death in the saint's bodily configuration contrasts admirably with the religious inspiration and hope in the saint's concentration on the host. The image of the world's grief is framed around the center of life, the saint's soul, which radiates from the center of the painting.

If Fromentin's analysis of *The Last Communion of St. Francis* is illuminating and positive, there are a number of analyses which are as instructive because of the weaknesses demonstrated in negative critiques. One can scarcely deny the judicious criticism of the dead man in *The Anatomy Lesson of Dr. Tulp* or the compositional weaknesses pointed out in *The Night Watch*, whatever one might think of the painting as a whole. Today Fromentin's appreciation of Potter is deemed generous, but his evaluation of the painter's famous painting, *The Young Bull*, is excellent in focusing on the young bull itself as the only object in the painting which is well conceived.

Among the individual chapters, the one on Frans Hals is especially excellent in its technical analysis and the chapter on Van Dyck is a literary gem. There Fromentin uses all his literary talents and the training he received as a writer in the *moraliste* tradition to create a brilliant portrait of the painter. In it he draws a composite view of the mundane painter mingling his own moral analysis with historical and biographical material to form a cameo image which is a mirror of the painter's work.

Some have noted that Fromentin's presentation of the concept of *valeurs* in colors is somewhat unclear. But his discussion of what it meant to be known as a colorist is excellent. Fromentin particularly emphasized the importance of nuance and the subtle use of colors as the significant factor. The critic distinguishes the term from *chiaroscuro*, a technique which he explores in reference to Rembrandt and which accounts for the concave nature of Dutch painting with its light at the center shrouded in shadows.

There is a long tradition in France of art criticism, some of the best written by literary masters such as Diderot, Gautier, Baudelaire, and Huysmans, to name a few of the most notable. Their work is appreciated because of their ability to recognize the greatness of the artists which would be singled out by posterity. Except for Baudelaire's discussion of color, there is little technical discussion of painting as an art. Fromentin does not share the burden of selecting the greatest artists of his own time. He only deals with contemporary painters in an oblique manner. In his book he accepts an even more rigorous challenge, that of evaluating the recognized masters. Fromentin dares to analyze the accepted canon honestly, to point out in specific terms what he considered the strengths and weaknesses of paintings long accepted as masterpieces or condemned as mediocre. The appreciation and hostility which the work elicits are evidence of its vitality even today.

CHAPTER 6

Fromentin and the Novel

I *Literary Influence*

WHEN Fromentin was asked to write a novel for the *Revue des Deux Mondes*, the psychological novel was not really in favor with the public. Stendhal and Balzac were already novelists of the past. *Madame Bovary* appeared in 1857 and the novel was on the verge of becoming more and more oriented toward society and determinism, just as painting had taken a decided turn toward objective naturalism. In a sense the form of the novel which Fromentin chose gives it a pastoral air[1] because it is more suitable to the circumstances of twenty years earlier. It gives the impression of being somewhat archaic itself. It might well have pleased the public of twenty-five years earlier when novels like Sainte-Beuve's *Volupté* (1834), Balzac's *Le Lys dans la vallée* (1835), and Musset's *Confessions d'un enfant du siècle* (1836) were more in vogue. Fromentin was especially fond of *Volupté*, which he had read numerous times. It is not difficult to see the relationship between Dominique's childhood and those of the principal characters in *Volupté* and *Le Lys dans la vallée*, nor is it strange that he was attracted by the romantic interest in these novels or the element of solitude and self-analysis. In fact, one should keep in mind that Fromentin's own love affair barely postdates these books by a few years. Although he was writing the story in 1860 the sentiments and associations were from twenty-five years earlier. It was already the story of another time and place and that was part of its charm for those who appreciated it.

In 1909 Georges Pailhès[2] attempted to prove that Fromentin had borrowed many of his most important scenes from Madame de Duras's novel *Edouard* (1825). Following Saint-Beuve's statement that the first one hundred pages of *Dominique* are the best, Pailhès develops the theory that these autobiographically based experiences were the only really original and inspired pages of the book. He felt that Fromentin, unable to write beyond what he had experienced personally, turned to Mme de Duras as a model for the remainder of his text. To support his argument he points to a number of important scenes[3] in the two novels which share a common feature or theme. What is striking, however, is that the scenes in question are so different. It is true that both novels have a scene in which the principal character goes to the lady's bedroom at night, but the tension in *Dominique* is completely absent from *Edouard*, where the two lovers have discussed their love and Mme de Nevers can find Edouard outside her room without being disturbed. And except for the involvement of flowers in one episode, the scenes compared by Pailhès are not really alike.[4] In fact, the importance of a social question in *Edouard*, the relationship between the lovers, and the attitude of the main character make the novels so different that, except for the mutual use of stock scenes, there is little to recommend the thesis of Pailhès. Actually, it is only the youthful upbringing of Edouard which truly reminds one of Dominique: he is the son of a respected provincial family, frequently visits their summer home, and expresses great love for solitude and nature. But one could establish such similarities with *Volupté* or *Le Lys dans la vallée* as well as other novels of the period.

The difficulty of establishing literary influence in a tradition which has a common heritage is well illustrated by Samuel Rhodes's suggestion that both Fromentin and Mme de Duras borrowed the stock scenes from *Valérie* (1803), the novel of Mme de Krüdener. In making his point Rhodes demonstrates how much closer to *Dominique* Mme de Krüdener's novel is in spirit and treatment of the scenes in question. Nevertheless, one is still not persuaded that there is more than a common tradition involved in the alleged borrowings, for it cannot be shown that Fromentin ever read the texts in question. Rhodes himself cites a number of other novels which resemble *Dominique* in various ways and one could add to his list. Lytton Sells[5] makes a strong case for the spiritual affinity between Senancour's relationship to Oberman and Fromentin's relationship to Dominique. He also illustrates a number of other *rapprochements* that one might make, including the central question concerning the quest for self-knowledge.

Recently Barbara Wright called attention to a rather striking resemblance between Armand du Mesnil's novel *Valdieu* (1860), dedicated to Fromentin, and *Dominique*.[6] Not only were the two men very close friends, but Fromentin constantly consulted du Mesnil on literary matters. Du Mesnil had great confidence in Fromentin's talent and Fromentin trusted du Mesnil's excellent taste and judgment. The literary critic, Edmond Schérer, recognized the affinity between the two novels. Wright speculates that the somewhat unsatisfactory conclusion of *Dominique* may well be the result of du Mesnil's experience. His novel ends melodramatically and was criticized for being overdrawn. Did Fromentin refuse a more romantically oriented conclusion because of a desire to avoid the problem du Mesnil had? One can do no better than to quote Professor Wright's own introductory statement:

Within a tradition like that of the French personal novel, direct literary "influences" are as elusive as the end of the rainbow, and just about as insubstantial when they are found.[7]

Not that the discussion of literary sources or influences is fruitless. To the contrary such studies add to our understanding of the "collective culture" and the "inherited framework" which formed the basis for the tradition of the personal novel in France.

II   *Résumé of* Dominique

The narrator begins by stating that the subject of his story is a man of middle age, a country gentleman content to live on his provincial estate in an existence which can be described as mediocre at best. Although he professes satisfaction with the mediocrity of his existence, there is some doubt whether M. de Bray is as content as he claims to be.

The narrator first meets Dominique de Bray while visiting a friend who lived in the vicinity of the de Bray estate. One autumn afternoon they encounter Dominique during his daily hunting expedition. At the end of their day of hunting, Dominique joins them and they accompany him back to the estate, where he is greeted warmly and joyously by his wife and two children. A few days later the narrator is invited to Dominique's. For the remainder of the season he visits regularly, though their friendship remains formal.

A year's absence intervenes. The narrator is asked to return once again during the harvest season. During this visit he becomes an intimate friend of the family. Dominique's life is filled by his numerous civic functions as mayor and by the care and support of the many tenants who live on his large estate. He fulfills his public duties with great patience, helping tenants and making daily rounds. He is clearly disturbed, however, when Père Jacques, an old servant who has been on the estate since Dominique was a child, stops him to reminisce. In addition to his habit of hunting alone Dominique occasionally retires to a room in the house which is filled with memorabilia, old papers, and souvenirs of the past. Even the walls are covered with numbers, dates, and phrases which were written a quarter of a century ago. During a visit to the room, Dominique reads poetry from one of the books to the narrator, who, when asked, criticizes it severely. To his embarrassment he learns that Dominique himself had written the verse in his youth. Dominique is not in the least offended by the criticism; in fact, he expresses the same opinion himself. The narrator is surprised to learn that he had also written (under a pseudonym) a political tract which had once received considerable attention. When questioned, Dominique comments that he had long since abandoned his literary ambitions.

At dinner they are visited by an old friend, a neighboring gentleman landowner who had known Dominique since adolescence. He is an elegant bachelor named Olivier d'Orsel, a mundane, personable individual who has deliberately withdrawn from any social contact, except for his occasional visits to the de Brays. After an active social existence in Paris, he now lives isolated on his provincial estate, filled with the ennui so typical of the nineteenth-century dandy. At dinner Mme de Bray and Olivier argue about the value of marriage as an institution and the merits of it in his own case. After the dinner Olivier departs for his own estate. A few days later a note arrives informing Dominique that Olivier has been injured. Dominique hurries to Olivier's estate, where he learns that his friend unsuccessfully attempted suicide, only succeeding in disfiguring himself.

The event causes Dominique to recount his own life to the narrator. Because he had lost his parents at a young age, Dominique was looked after by his father's sister, Mme Ceyssac, a devout and kind woman. She provided him with a good tutor, a serious, upright, and diligent young man named Augustin. Not truly gifted, Augustin nonetheless had ambitions for a career of his own and worked ceaselessly to rise from his lowly condition to prominence. He was fond of Dominique and sought to instill in him the perseverance and discipline necessary for success. Dominique was a good student, sensitive to the beauty of nature and literature. At sixteen he was prepared for the *lycée* at Ormesson, where he met the young, carefree Olivier, a student who was bored with studies and did not like associating with a bourgeois class which he considered inferior and which shared none of his tastes. Through Olivier Dominique met Julie and Madeleine, Olivier's cousins. The four became good friends.

A year passed. Dominique spent his time in such self-scrutiny that he was miserable. One day when he was out walking (during his seventeenth year) a kind of crisis developed. During the evening walk, he unexpectedly met Olivier, Madeleine, and Julie. Not wishing to see anyone and suddenly embarrassed, Dominique greeted them and left precipitously. The following Sunday at dinner he felt the need to change from his usual seat next to Madeleine. He saw her for the first time in a new way and realized that she was the cause of the disturbed state in which he found himself.

A few weeks later M. d'Orsel, Madeleine, and Julie left for a period of two months. Dominique liked the security of the household without the danger of her presence, yet enjoyed going to the places where he usually saw her. On one occasion he even visited her room and experienced great pleasure, as if it held her presence. When Olivier returned, the two departed together. Olivier surprised Dominique by confiding in him concerning his amorous affairs.

Madeleine arrived toward the end of July. Dominique noticed a considerable change in her. He had never before realized the vast difference between one eighteen and one seventeen. Now he was aware that Madeleine seemed older. In the baggage he noticed, but paid little attention to, a bouquet of rhododendrons sent by Count Alfred de Nièvres.

Some time passed. One day Dominique discovered that the family was absent. They remained away for three days. When they returned, Dominique immediately went to see them. The family were all gathered along with the Count de Nièvres. Suddenly it dawned on Dominique that Madeleine was about to be married and that he had lost her.

For some time he spent his days away from the d'Orsel family. A week before the wedding Madeleine spoke to Dominique in private to persuade him that their friendship should remain unchanged and that she counted on him to be a friend to her future husband.

Dominique escorted Julie to the wedding and suffered through a miserable day and night, the realization of his situation becoming clearer and more devastating as time passed.

Madeleine returned in time to be present at Dominique's graduation awards ceremony. Dominique was disturbed by her presence, embarrassed that the discrepancy in their roles should be thus emphasized. It was a moment he long remembered. Soon after Olivier and Dominique left for Paris. It was not long before Dominique felt himself very much alone. Although he had found Augustin again, his former tutor had his own life to live and Olivier soon began an existence which coincided little with his own. After he had observed his misery and solitude for some months, Olivier impatiently scolded Dominique for living like a hermit just because of Madeleine. Although he admitted that it might not be possible to stop loving Madeleine, he insisted that he replace her in his life with someone else.

Dominique passed some time with Augustin. When Dominique asked him if he were happy, he responded that he had posed the wrong question. An honest man can only be expected to do all he can to be happy. Whether or not his efforts are rewarded lies beyond his control. His advice to Dominique was different from Olivier's. He urged him to begin to participate in life, the only sure way to overcome his grief. Some time later Dominique met Olivier, who was accompanied by two women. Dominique began an affair with the young woman he met through Olivier. Two months later, when he heard that Madeleine would be returning to Ormesson, he ended the affair and returned there himself.

During the two autumn months which he passed near Madeleine, the five young people spent much time together. Dominique recalls a number of memorable occasions, among them the famous climb to the top of the lighthouse and their last day before returning to Paris.

At Paris Dominique could not hope to have Madeleine's undivided attention, even though she assured him that she would always be home to him. At her request he attended a ball she gave but soon became miserable, jealous to see her playing the role of Mme de Nièvres and dressed in the seductive attire of Parisian society.

In the weeks that followed, Dominique became more and more disturbed by their relationship. He resented it and sought to become more explicit in his comments to force Madeleine to recognize his feelings. Unsuccessful, Dominique stayed away from Madeleine's for

a few weeks. Then he precipitously decided to visit her, determined
to avow his love. The situation progressed from one of strained
emotion to anguish. Before their meeting had the opportunity to
become more compromising than it already had, Madeleine left the
room.

The next time Dominique saw Madeleine his attitude was so
changed that she was able to relax her guard, to treat him as if the
previous scene had never occurred. When he tried to apologize
sometime later, Madeleine urged him to be silent and to cure himself. She vowed to help him and spent much time with him thereafter.
Her attempts to help him conquer his passion only led to a situation of
greater intimacy between them. After a time Madeleine departed on
vacation to Germany. She insisted that Dominique not follow her and
not write, although she wrote to him to ease his misery somewhat.
When she returned, Dominique announced that he himself was
going to leave on an extended trip to Italy. Although he had planned a
trip of several months, he returned after only a few weeks. In her
feeling of guilt over Dominique's miserable condition, Madeleine
seemed determined to undo what she felt she had done. She spent
more and more time with Dominique, even arranging rendezvous
outside her own home, a step which both recognized to be dangerous
for her reputation and marriage. Dominique enjoyed the intimacy,
but not without remorse. He was not unmindful that Madeleine drew
nearer and nearer to the danger she sought to avoid. One day
Dominique pretended that Madeleine had succeeded in her cure,
that he no longer loved her. The cruelty of his comment was immediately apparent. Madeleine was greatly affected by the statement. Dominique suggested that they might be better off not to see
one another. At a certain point Madeleine ceased her mission of cure.
Her attitude changed. She became moody, unpredictable in her
behavior, and withdrew from Dominique's company.

During this period of anguish and joy, Dominique had remained in
touch with Augustin, whose labors were bringing him some measure
of success. Now he learned that Augustin had married. He invited
Dominique to meet his wife. Dominique had mixed emotions in
seeing the poor living conditions of the household: there were no
servants and Augustin himself had to help with many of the daily
chores. Yet Augustin's contentment with his wife and companion
revealed to Dominique a satisfaction with his situation which took

away the depressing aspect of Augustin's lower-middle-class economic condition. When he told Olivier of Augustin's marriage,
Olivier replied scornfully concerning the ability of the poor to make
themselves even more miserable. Olivier was more sarcastic than
usual, undoubtedly affected by the knowledge that Julie had seen
him with someone else and was probably depressed. Dominique
visited Madeleine to discover the truth. He found Julie indisposed
and surmised that her illness was caused by the appearance of Olivier
with someone else. When Dominique confronted Olivier with the
opinion that he might be happier were he to marry Julie, Olivier
exploded in a rather caustic reply concerning the "benefits" of marriage. He even predicted that Madeleine would one day fall into
Dominique's arms and that he would not even take advantage of the
situation. Olivier concluded his speech with the realistically depressing assessment that men were not meant to have pure happiness on
earth and must be content with something less. For his part he
wished that someone could render the greatest service to man by
killing ennui. The two friends parted. Although their friendship was
not broken, Dominique recognized that they would never again be
intimate friends.

It had been more than a month since Dominique had had the
opportunity to be with Madeleine for more than five minutes. A
chance encounter brought them together. Worried that she might be
seen, Madeleine separated from Dominique quickly, but invited him
to join her at the opera. During the performance Dominique was
ecstatic to be so near Madeleine and thought that he perceived signs
that her will to resist him was virtually gone. He subsequently tried
to see her but she refused, finally telling him so in a note.

Dominique then changed his life entirely, adopting a new circle of
friends and activities. He read voraciously and led a more active
existence when not reading. After a few months he went through the
verse he had written in his youth, made two volumes of poetry, added
a preface, and published them anonymously. Having taken care of his
past, Dominique entered the political world with the notion that he
would become useful after so many unproductive years. In the back of
his mind he hoped to find Madeleine again, but only after he had
acquired some reputation. Under a fictitious name he wrote two
moderately successful books on politics which brought him to the
threshold of fame. His critical nature intervened, however, and he

made a serious assessment of his own talents. In his own judgment he could not be too optimistic: he had to face the fact that his work was basically mediocre.

Meanwhile, during the two-year absence he had kept up with news concerning Madeleine through conversations with Olivier and Augustin. On one such occasion he learned from Olivier that Julie was seriously ill and that Madeleine had not been well either. He decided that he could no longer stay away and the next day went to Nièvres. It was November. Madeleine and Dominique spent three days together. On the third day Madeleine insisted that Dominique accompany her on a long ride in the woods. The next day when they were together folding her shawl, Madeleine fell into Dominique's arms. Dominique did not take advantage of her. Later Madeleine admitted her love for Dominique, but only after she had told him that they must never see one another again. Dominique departed on the following day and went to Augustin, where he found his former tutor prospering with wife and child and busy at work. Before returning to Villeneuve and Trembles, Dominique saw Olivier, who was leaving France, and visited Mme Ceyssac at Ormesson. When he arrived at Trembles, his first encounter was with old André, the servant he had known since childhood. At this point Dominique's story was complete.

The narrator sees Dominique in his new life committed to the service of his family and those who live about him. As Dominique says to his friend, Olivier seems to have lost his struggle with his old enemy, ennui. As they are talking a carriage arrives. It is Augustin paying a visit to his friend, Dominique.

III *Autobiographical Content*

The fulfillment of Fromentin's aspirations as a writer came late in his career yet was not entirely unexpected. He had become known earlier by his travel accounts, *Un Eté dans le Sahara* and *Une Année dans le Sahel*. Fromentin was recognized for his excellent use of the language and careful style, so it is not surprising that, given the opportunity presented by François Buloz, he should write a novel about his own youthful romance. It is common enough for novelists to begin their careers with a quasi-autobiographical novel and it was even more prevalent among the Romantic writers of the early nineteenth century. Although Fromentin was not contemplating such a novel when asked by Buloz, the idea was not entirely new to him. In fact, shortly after Jenny's death in 1844 he had vowed to write their story:

Amie, ma divine et sainte amie, je veux et vais écrire notre histoire commune, depuis le premier jour jusqu'au dernier. Et chaque fois qu'un souvenir effacé luira subitement dans ma mémoire, chaque fois qu'un mot plus tendre et plus ému jaillira de mon coeur, ce seront autant de marques pour moi que tu m'entends . . . .[8]

Yet the immediate effect of her death seems to have been the end of his interest in poetry. Whether because the experience was too painful for him to write about or because his interest in painting drew him away from any serious consideration of fulfilling the vow, Fromentin never returned to the idea. For most writers the fifteen years which had intervened would present certain difficulties. In some ways the situation was ideal for Fromentin's method of artistic creation, given the importance of memory in his aesthetic and in his creative effort.

In this sense one would be wrong to look for a chronological presentation of his youthful romance with Jenny-Caroline-Léocadie Chessé, the Madeleine of his novel. What one finds, rather, is a transformed version of their relationship. Thus one can study the autobiographical reality of the novel on more than one level. One can find people, events, and places which correspond to those in Fromentin's own life and the transpositions and transformations which he made of them. One can also study the interior development of the principal character and relate this to what we know about Fromentin himself. But the difficulty in such an analysis involves the question of sincerity on the one hand and fictional needs on the other. One cannot be certain what belongs to Dominique as the principal character within a novelistic framework and what can be seen as a reflection of Fromentin's own nature. The following analysis presents the relationship between the novel and Fromentin's own life. The setting, events, and characters will be analyzed with a view toward elucidating the autobiographical content of the text and the basic alterations which Fromentin made in adapting them to a fictional setting.

As Camille Reynaud[9] pointed out more than forty years ago, only the first nine chapters really follow Fromentin's life in its broad outline. One can see in the generally solitary, provincial upbringing of Dominique, followed by his journey to Paris for further study, the basic outline of Fromentin's early schooling. Within that outline, Dominique's love for a girl older than he follows Fromentin's own experience, though not in detail. Chapters 11 and 12 probably represent his own fictional version of vacations spent at Saint Maurice. In the remainder of the novel, there is no parallel for the events in Fromentin's life.

In the introductory chapters one notes many things which relate to Fromentin's youth. The setting at Trembles is clearly drawn from Fromentin's favorite estate, Vaugoin,[10] and the emphasis on autumn and its activities reflect Fromentin's own expressed predilection for that season of the year. When Dominique goes to Ormesson to visit his aunt, Mme Ceyssac, one finds her home to be that of his own childhood in La Rochelle.[11]

Thus the setting for the first half of the novel is clearly drawn from his own background, but how closely can the characters be identified with friends and acquaintances of Fromentin's youth? One can see the element of autobiography and how Fromentin altered reality in comparing Dominique with the author. Dominique's serious, self-analytical nature certainly reminds one of the Fromentin one sees in his correspondence. When Dominique evaluates his own poetry and political writings, the severity of judgment is characteristic of Fromentin's assessment of his own work. In fact, the basic philosophy of the book, with the emphasis placed on self knowledge and the importance of making an honest evaluation of one's role, contribution, and talent, accord well with Fromentin's own outlook.

There are some notable differences, however, between Fromentin and Dominique. Fromentin also renounced poetry but he never took any active interest in politics. Again Dominique considered his talents meager and withdrew despite the success of his two books and a growing reputation. Fromentin knew success in two areas: as a painter and as a writer of travel literature. He realized his own limitations as a painter and even felt that his lasting contribution would be more notable as a writer.[12] Nevertheless, he never really ceased painting. Although Dominique is a sensitive, thoughtful human being with a poetic side to his personality, he is far more practical in orientation than Fromentin. Perhaps the role of country gentleman was Fromentin's way of expressing the need to accept one's own limited talents and capabilities in order to find the peaceful happiness he set as a goal. But in his own life nothing ever replaced his focus on art and his striving to reproduce on canvas or in prose the essence of the interesting and beautiful things he saw. One cannot help but feel that Fromentin had a more poetic nature than his autobiographical counterpart and that, despite his romantic attachment and vivid memory, he lived more wholly in the present. Dominique attempts to leave the past behind, to find happiness in an active contribution to the present. The novel never really escapes a heavy sense of regret. The past remains a burden on the present, although Fromentin intended the reader to feel that he had reached an understanding of himself and was content. In Fromentin's own life one feels that the past was laid to rest, that it remained compartmentalized in the artist's memory and no longer affected his present state of mind.

Dominique's wife is identified with Marie Cavellet de Beaumont, Fromentin's spouse. It is difficult to get a good picture of Marie from the published correspondence. However, the assertive wife of Dominique who lectures Olivier for his failure to give of himself to life strikes me as far more aggressive than Fromentin's own wife.

Olivier d'Orsel was identified by Fromentin himself as being modeled on his childhood friend and neighbor, Léon Mouliade. This is revealed in a letter dated October 1875, written shortly after Fromentin had seen his old friend after an interval of nearly thirty years:

Imaginez-vous qu'hier j'ai revu ici, chez moi, entrant comme un revenant, mon vieil ami de jeunesse, l'Olivier de *Dominique* . . . . Il a quitté la Vendée, vendu toutes ses terres, et s'est retiré pour mourir en paix . . . au fond de la Bretagne, en Finistère, en pleine forêt, dans un château qu'il a reconstruit, mais auquel il laisse son nom celtique et son titre de manoir. Il n'y est pas *tout à fait seul*. Il n'a jamais été tout à fait seul, mon Olivier. Toujours le même; mais c'est la même solitude morale. Au fond, le même ennui, la même douceur élégante et désabusée, finalement la même idée fausse de la vie.[13]

Léon and Eugène were friends in youth and attended the same school in La Rochelle. Léon's parents were large landowners at Fontenay-le-Comte some fifty miles from La Rochelle. Mouliade went to Paris in 1839 and Fromentin joined him in 1840. In 1842 they passed their vacation together in La Rochelle. Fromentin made of Olivier an example of the lost Romantic figure and used him to represent one of the tendencies or drives in his own character. The ennui-filled dandy played a large role in the literature he admired. Paul Bataillard's comment well expresses the feeling which Fromentin and the "last generation of Romantics" had:

Nous étions en réalité les derniers fils des Werther, des René, des Adolphe, des Obermann, des Amaury, auxquels on peut ajouter le Rousseau des *Confessions* . . . .[14]

There has been no truly successful identification of Augustin, in the sense that no single acquaintance of Fromentin clearly fills the role. Barbara Wright is probably correct in stating that Augustin is a synthesis of several personalities.[15] For Dominique's tutor some have suggested Léopold Delayant, librarian and historian, one of Fromentin's teachers at La Rochelle.[16] For certain aspects of Augustin, his role of advisor and confidant, Professor Wright proposes Paul Bataillard, Fromentin's close friend of more than thirty years. Not only was Bataillard about four years older than Fromentin, but his career corresponds more nearly with Augustin's. However, his personality differed considerably from the latter's, especially in the condition of Augustin's material existence and his laborious, workman-like career. Probably the most likely model for Augustin was Emile Beltrémieux,[17] Fromentin's close friend until his rather sudden death in 1848. He was a few years older than Fromentin and had studied medicine at Paris with Charles, Fromentin's brother. Beltrémieux went to the capital in 1836 and wrote serious letters of advice to Fromentin concerning Paris and what to expect when he came. He worked diligently in many areas including drama, poetry, and translation. An insatiable reader, he loved Byron, Shakespeare, history, the classics, and the Romantic novel. Just like Augustin he was very active in politics and entered journalism. In a letter to Lilia Beltrémieux shortly after her brother's death, Fromentin refers to Emile's study as their sanctuary, a kind of room of memories such as he created for Dominique in the novel.

It was not until 1926 that the model for Madeleine was disclosed to the general public as the creole neighbor, Jenny Chessé, a childhood playmate nearly four years older than the novelist. Jenny married a tax collector named Emile Béraud in October 1834 when she was seventeen. She remained married to Emile Béraud until her death from cancer in 1844. Because of the age difference, limited to one year in the novel, it is unlikely that Fromentin could have had any romantic inclinations toward Jenny prior to her marriage.

Thus one can see that the novel by no means produces a historical account of Fromentin's early years. For the sake of *vraisemblance*, Fromentin made Dominique only a year younger than Madeleine and already in love with her, although he only comes .to realize it when she marries. Fromentin's love for Jenny probably dates from 1837, some three years after the marriage. It could be that Jenny was present at his graduation awards ceremony in 1838 (just as in the novel), but it is not certain. What is certain is that he became a regular visitor to the Béraud home, even during M. Béraud's absence. The situation caused a scandal in the town, despite the presence at their meetings of a third party, identified as Lilia Beltrémieux by Camille Reynaud, who suggested that Lilia was herself in love with Fromentin. In fact, Lilia is probably the Julie of the novel, the parallel victim of an impossible love. It is even thought that Jenny may have imagined marrying Lilia to Fromentin, an idea found in the novel.

Those who have reported concerning Jenny's personality do not paint a very flattering picture of her. She struck Fromentin's friends as a rather superficial person, somewhat selfish and demanding. She was perceived as being coquettish and temperamental, not at all like the modest, sensitive woman in the novel. However, one cannot completely trust these evaluations of the young creole, for it is not likely that the sources, given the circumstances, would be well disposed toward her. In any case Fromentin's Madeleine is undoubtedly an idealization, recast to fit the needs of the fictional reality. Although it is not really known whether Fromentin and Jenny became lovers,[18] Sainte-Beuve suggested in his review that the true love affair could not have remained so chaste as that in the novel. In the introduction to her edition, Barbara Wright states that letters not available to the public indicate that the love between Fromentin and Jenny did not remain Platonic. In the novel Fromentin focused his attention upon Madeleine's attempt to avoid adultery despite her love for Dominique and the inattention of her husband. It is important to the dramatic action that the reader be persuaded of Madeleine's need to remain pure. Only if one accepts the importance of Madeleine's integrity can Dominique's own response seem psychologically valid. Thus the reality, whatever it was, is not so important in shaping Madeleine's personality as the fictional setting which Fromentin created.[19]

CHAPTER 7

Narrative Structures in Dominique

I The Frame Story

*D*OMINIQUE is the narrative account of selected moments drawn from the adolescence and youth of the book's principal character. Because of the novel's meaning, it is important that this period in Dominique's life not be seen in isolation but rather in comparison to the life being led by the principal character more than twenty years later. Thus Fromentin chose to present the novel in the form of a frame story—one might say, in this case, a story within a setting. The narration of Dominique's youth occupies chapters 3 through 17 and has its own structural unity, since neither the beginning nor the end is chronologically linked to the frame story. Chapters 1, 2, and 18 provide a kind of prologue and epilogue to the main narrative but are really much more important to the novel's meaning than the usual frame story, which is often a technical convenience for the author.

In *Dominique* the first two chapters have their own inner logic and are as important to the novel as the retrospective narrative. Since the narrator will relate an experience which he had more than two decades earlier, the reader has many questions pertaining to the veracity of the account and the narrator's perspective. Moreover, because of Dominique's ambivalent character, the reader is eager to know what kind of person he has become since his youth. The frame narrator, who introduces one to Dominique, lends objectivity to the account. Like the reader he is an unbiased observer who can comment independently on Dominique's account, but, more importantly, he reflects on whether the narrator's account is corroborated by what he knows or whether the narrator's own demeanor accords with what has been said.

In these three frame chapters, then, one must see a full picture of Dominique as he is at the time he begins his narrative. The first chapter is economical in accomplishing this. It begins with a quotation from Dominique in which he assesses his current life, followed

by the narrator's comments on the objectivity and truth of his statement. This brief introduction is followed by scenes which present the
two aspects of Dominique's existence. When we first see Dominique,
he is hunting and alone. The reader is told that he hunts regularly and
always insists on being alone. However, to dispel any thoughts that
Dominique is antisocial or ill-tempered, the author shows his courte-
ous treatment of the other hunters and the happy affection displayed
by his family in greeting him.

Chapter 2 continues to broaden our knowledge of Dominique's life
within the provincial setting. We see him surrounded by a happy
family and busily engaged in running an estate of contented tenants.
Dominique's civil and private obligations fill his day with activities
necessary to those who live in the region. Yet this is not the only
picture which the author draws. He is disturbed on his rides by Père
Jacques, who insists on recalling the old days whenever he encounters Dominique. And when rain interrupts his round of activities, he
withdraws alone to a room filled with memorabilia, its walls covered
with dates, numbers, and phrases written at an earlier time. It is clear
that the room is symbolic of another time or side of Dominique's
character and that his withdrawal there relates to his solitary hunting
expeditions and may be related to his annoyance at Père Jacques'
reminiscences.

Thus Fromentin uses the two frame chapters to develop the seem-
ing disparity between the happy, serene public figure and the man
who often prefers to be alone in nature or in his room of memories.
One has the impression that his life has not always been so ordered or
happy as it now appears. In addition to this presentation, the author
introduces one of the main characters of the inner narrative and
develops a conversation concerning marriage which is vital to the
text's meaning and plays the role of catalyst in the novel. After the
disturbing dinner discussion concerning the importance of leading a
useful life, Olivier returns home and attempts suicide. It is this event
which causes Dominique to retire to his room with his new friend and
recount the story of his youth.

At the conclusion of Dominique's narrative, the scene is again the
special room with the enigmatic wall-writings. Fromentin chose not
to lengthen the novel at this point to provide a transition between the
events of the past and Dominique's current life.[1] In fact he returns to
the scene just as he had left it, except that the shadows have begun to
darken the walls of the room, as if closing out the past time which had
been drawn into the present momentarily by the magic of memory.

Sounds of the family and noises of the general activity from outside the room begin to invade the quiet of the inner sanctum. Without answering the many questions which one might ask in an effort to link past and present, Fromentin quickly ends the story, but not without a brief indication which helps to tie the inner narrative to Dominique's current life. He refers to the suicide attempt of Olivier as if it had closed a final chapter of the history: he had lost his long battle with life and ennui. Finally, the arrival of Augustin on the book's final page indicates that his former tutor's influence and example continue to play a prominent role in Dominique's life.

II   *The Inner Narrative*

Chapters 3 through 17 contain the narrative of Dominique's youthful love affair with Madeleine and his subsequent return to Trembles. In a sense the central focus of the narrative is Madeleine's wedding in chapter 7. What precedes pertains to the awakening of love and what follows concerns the grief and conflict brought about by the impossible situation created by Madeleine's marriage.

In chapters 3 through 5 Dominique recounts his early years at Trembles and Ormesson. The narrator does not attempt to provide a detailed history of these years; rather he focuses on one element in growing up which relates to the central drama of the story. In chapter 3 he sets the stage of his early life, how he grew up without parents, and learned to love nature. To his rather undisciplined existence came his tutor, Augustin, a young man as methodical and diligent as Dominique was carefree. After these two portraits, the chapter closes with the final lesson which Augustin assigned, the Latin composition concerning Hannibal's departure from Italy. The assignment fills Dominique with a level of emotion scarcely appropriate for the passage. It is an indication that something new is stirring in the young Dominique, who is about to enter a new phase of life both in terms of his education and emotional development.

In chapter 4 Dominique departs for Ormesson, where he will pursue his formal education. The nature of life in the somber, middle-class town contrasts sharply with the rural, carefree existence which had typified Trembles. At Ormesson Dominique meets Olivier and his two cousins, Julie and Madeleine. At this point all of the principal characters have been introduced.

Dominique recognizes that a change is occurring in him, but he is unable to identify it. He wishes to be alone in his room or in the country by himself. He tries to avoid his friends. In this solitary setting chapter 6 includes two meaningful encounters, both with Madeleine. As Dominique recalls his own feelings at the time, he is careful to emphasize that he was totally unaware of the reason for his disquietude. During one of his solitary walks he unexpectedly encounters Madeleine, Julie and Olivier. Caught at an awkward moment, he hastens to leave them, even though he has no real excuse to offer. Later at the dinner table he unaccountably exchanges his customary seat next to Madeleine for one across the table. Only after this scene does it begin to dawn on him that his emotional disturbance involves Madeleine.[2]

Just as Dominique begins to recognize his special feeling for Madeleine, the novel moves quickly to the two chapters which precipitate the crisis in his life. Chapters 6 and 7 present a sharp contrast with the meandering, introspective character of the preceding chapters. Fromentin expresses this by contrasting Dominique's own feeling of timelessness as he is beset by alternating feelings of ecstasy, fear, and grief. His own emotional state and ignorance of reality make him unaware that life proceeds within strict temporal limits. The principal event in chapter 6 occurs in the final scene, when Dominique is jolted by the realization that Madeleine is being engaged and that this moment, which he is allowed to witness only from the outside, changes the nature of his own existence completely. The contrast between Dominique's timeless, adolescent world and the finite world which Madeleine has just entered is cleverly presented in the chapter. At the beginning Dominique is relieved to hear that M. d'Orsel has taken his daughter on a two-month vacation. Dominique even laments that two months may not be enough time for him to collect himself. Yet he takes joy in knowing that he can reflect on Madeleine, pass time near her home, and even enter her room without fearing the uncomfortable encounters which embarrass him and threaten to reveal his feelings. He is unaware that Madeleine is entering a process which takes only a certain time to complete and that her departure signals the beginning of the procedure.

The engagement scene has the effect of crystallizing everything for Dominique. Not only is he able to identify his feeling for Madeleine as love, but he is brought abruptly out of his adolescent world into the grown-up reality which he must come to share.

In chapter 7 there is only one event of importance: Madeleine is married amid the mixed joy and indifference of such occasions, while the shocked Dominique stares at the event, again an observer and not a true participant, excruciatingly aware of the contrast between his inner thoughts and feelings and the noisy turmoil of the celebration.

The following three chapters follow two developments in the novel. Subsequent to the wedding, including the remainder of chapter 7, Dominique suffers the grief which comes with his realization of what the marriage really means to his life. But it is also a period which marks a substantial change in his own maturity. Essentially he makes the transition from being a schoolboy to a person once again the equal of Madeleine. Earlier she had crossed the fine line which divides the young girl from the adult. Although only a year younger than Madeleine, Dominique remains for a brief time in the adolescent world. At this moment the year's difference separates them by an insurmountable barrier. Fromentin illustrates this in the graduation ceremony which Madeleine attends. It is a moment Dominique dreads because his academic garments are symbolic of the gulf which separates him from Mme de Nièvres. He is painfully conscious of the disparity between them and is reluctant to see her. Yet when the ceremony ends and he descends to accept congratulations, it is Madeleine who is embarrassed and blushes at the encounter. Dominique has crossed the threshold of adolescence and is prepared to take on the role of a young man.

Chapter 9 presents Dominique at Paris, living the life of the young romantic who is hopelessly in love and pours out his lovelorn emotions in poetry. He writes feverishly, persuaded that he has the genius of the gifted poet. It is a period of debate in his life and his two friends, Olivier and Augustin, begin to occupy a larger role in the novel's structure. Both offer him advice about life. Olivier urges him to replace his interest in Madeleine by feminine companionship. Chapters 9 and 10 present the conflicting advice of his two mentors. At the end of chapter 10 he joins Olivier at the opera and begins a two-month affair.

This is a turning point in the novel. Dominique has been torn between the advice of Olivier and Augustin. In deciding to follow Olivier he begins a way of life which he quickly realizes cannot bring him satisfaction and fulfillment. Because of his dissatisfaction, he immediately seizes the opportunity to return to Trembles when he learns that Madeleine plans to vacation there. Trembles represents the security and happiness of his youth; he can return to his origins and begin again in the recovered friendship of Madeleine. Because Trembles is his childhood home, many of the current obstacles can be overlooked, as if removed by stepping back into a period in which they did not exist.

Chapters 11 through 13 develop a growing love and intimacy between Dominique and Madeleine. Once again Dominique lives in the timeless setting of his childhood. Just as in the earlier section he lives the summer, oblivious of time, as if the moment would never end. The famous lighthouse scene marks the sensual element which has entered their relationship, a factor which had not been present in their earlier childhood intimacy. The final walk with Madeleine recreates the clash between the timeless nature of their love and the exigencies of time which the real world imposes. Just as the wedding must follow the engagement after a certain time, so must the summer of love end with the close of autumn. The realities of winter and marriage must be faced.

However, the development in chapters 11 through 13 shifts focus somewhat. Whereas chapters 3 through 5 traced the awakening of love in Dominique, chapters 11 through 13 focus on Madeleine, who is unaware or does not wish to recognize that her friendship with Dominique is changing. In the remainder of the narrative Dominique tries to discover Madeleine's real feelings for him and then tries to force her to acknowledge that she loves him. Just as Dominique avoided admitting to himself his real problem, so does Madeleine attempt to hide and overcome her true feelings. After the pastoral interlude at Trembles, the scene changes to Paris and the social life of Madeleine's new world.

The contrast between chapters 11 and 12 is illustrated vividly in the ball scene, the initial moment of the latter chapter. Both Dominique and Madeleine have left the innocent days of childhood and the asensual friendship of an earlier time. Dominique is disturbed by the mundane surroundings and offended by the revealing cut of Madeleine's gown. The ball begins a rather cruel game of chess by Dominique as he alternates seduction and abandonment in an effort to force Madeleine to confess her love. When intimate conversations fail to produce the desired confession, Dominique leaves for a month and returns precipitously to find a grieving, tortured Madeleine. Finally Madeleine makes the fatal mistake of entering into complicity, ostensibly promising herself only to help Dominique recover his former self. Chapter 13 traces the growing intimacy of the two lovers, helped by the fiction that Madeleine is really seeing him so regularly to be of help. The nobility of her cause helps her ignore the prudent barriers imposed by social convention as she agrees to see him away from her home when his visits become noticeably regular.

At this point the novel might well be arriving at the crisis it reaches in chapter 17, except for Dominique's inner urge to force Madeleine to avow her love openly. As a kind of cruel joke Dominique announces to Madeleine that she has been successful in her cure, that he no longer loves her. The shock is so great to her, despite his immediate disavowal of the remark, that he still finds her character altered the next day.

Dominique's remark has the effect of delaying the development of the novel. The pause in the progress of their love allows Fromentin to focus once again on the direction which Dominique's life is taking. Chapter 14 is an interlude within the structure of the romance. While Dominique spends half of the chapter with Augustin and the other half with Olivier, the affair with Madeleine remains suspended. However, within another framework, discussed in the next chapter, the outcome of chapter 14 is decisive in Dominique's life and really determines his future. In some ways it is the climax of the book, the resolution of a long inner struggle. More than any other single chapter this one links the events of the past to Dominique's present way of life. At its conclusion one can see the logic in Dominique's current existence and how the philosophical assumptions which underlie his present life are related to the events of the past.

In a sense chapter 15 forms a transition to the long two-year break from Madeleine in the following chapter. The development of Dominique into manhood is nearly complete. He is overjoyed now that he feels certain that Madeleine loves him and is sure that she cannot resist him. After a month's absence, Madeleine meets him in the street and invites him to the opera. At the performance Dominique sits close to Madeleine and is intoxicated by the combination of music and fragrance from her perfume. The effect on Madeleine is not so apparent until they return and Madeleine's comments while holding the bouquet reflect the extent that she feels tortured by Dominique. In this last scene the emphasis on the increasingly sensual nature of their relationship prepares the reader for the wild ride of chapter 17 and the ultimate break between them.

On the one hand, chapter 16 provides the necessary separation of the two lovers prior to the dramatic denouement of the story. Thus it serves as a transition chapter within the framework of their romance. On the other hand, it is a chapter of great significance in the long development of Dominique from the sheltered, young child through adolescence to maturity. In his relationship to Madeleine he has reached full maturity and the sexual drive which that implies. Now the reader sees an energetic young man ambitiously testing his talents in the world at large. First he ventures into the world of poetry and then turns to the political arena. This activity brings considerable success and even some visibility as a rising young writer and critic of the political scene. However, he becomes disenchanted with the superficial nature of this activity and, when Olivier tells him that Julie is ill, he seizes the opportunity to visit Madeleine and her family after a two-year absence.

This final encounter between Madeleine and Dominique brings to a climax the development of their relationship as lovers (which began in chapter 11). The sequence of five chapters is interrupted only by the two interludes (chapters 14 and 16) in which Dominique chooses between Olivier and Augustin and develops his active life. The love affair has been prepared for such a climax since chapter 13. The delay has the effect of allowing both Madeleine and Dominique to become older and less subject to the fears of adolescence. Madeleine has been married long enough for M. de Nièvres not to react to her letter that Dominique has arrived, except to say that he will remain absent another month.

The chapter can be divided into three principal scenes: the wild ride in the forest, the joining of the shawl, and their last conversation together. Like the scene in the lighthouse, the wild ride through the forest represents the repressed sexual attraction which lies just beneath the surface. The ride has the obvious characteristics which relate to their love affair: Dominique mounts on M. de Nièvres's horse, rides off the path, thus putting him in great danger from low branches, and Madeleine leads the chase at a wild pace. Dominique describes the ride as a duel between two who seem more enemies than friends, an obvious reference to the adversary relationship which they have had since chapter 12. After the ride Madeleine retires to her room. The next day Dominique announces that he will leave. The imminent threat of his departure causes the lovers to spend the day together. This leads to the incident with the shawl and Madeleine's symbolic capitulation. That evening Madeleine asks to see Dominique alone. She makes the long awaited confession that she loves him. She can now admit as much openly, since she has told him that she will never see him again.

III *The Circular Journey*

In Fromentin's own life travel played a large role in his artistic formation. Despite his love of the region in which he was born, it is evident from his correspondence that he came ⸱⸱ feel out of place among the people of the area and even in his own family circle. A professional artistic career was far too impractical to gain the approval of his family or the inhabitants of the region. One might paint or write as an additional interest, but one must have a real profession to establish financial security and respect. For Fromentin his study at Paris gave him the independence he needed to engage in an artistic career. Even in the choice of studio one can see the extent of the constraint imposed on the young artist, as his father insisted on one of the most traditional schools of painting then active. The avant-garde of the time lay in the rising interest in objective realism. Because of his temperament and aesthetic values, such an attitude toward art could never hold much appeal for the young painter. Basically he agreed with his father's own aesthetic values. He believed in the value of studying and imitating the masters; yet he knew that he must find his own subject matter and style if he were to make his mark among the best painters of the day. North Africa had become the subject of several painters of the past decade whose work had caught his attention. When the opportunity came to travel to North Africa, he took it, even though he had to leave in secrecy and without his family's blessing.

Arthur Evans sees in his trip to North Africa a kind of archetypal voyage to the unknown.[3] *Un Eté* represents for him a kind of epic portrayal of this adventure, whereas *Une Année* has more of a pastoral mood. The characterization is not without value. The northern portion of the continent, with its vast, mysterious desert, represented a new frontier for the nineteenth-century Frenchman. Much is often said about Fromentin's fascination with the great expanse of the horizon, but it is noted that he prefers a horizon that has limits. This is seen as a basic element in his personality and artistic perspective.

There is some truth in this; however, Fromentin's trip to the edge of the desert was fascinating to him in part because of the unknown reaches which lay beyond. As pointed out in chapter 4, Fromentin saw in the enigmatic reaches of the silent desert an image of the inner self. In that respect he enjoyed the quiet, reflective solitude. He had no interest in exploring the desert as did Vandell, his companion in *Une Année*. His classic view of reality told him that, though the shapes and forms might indeed be bizarre, the inner reality of human nature and existence would not be different. He could learn as much examining the enigmatic self which so resembled the silent desert. In *Une Année* he expresses this idea well when he states that he will not travel so much this time. Instead he will place himself and observe the world as it passes by:

C'est à mon avis le meilleur moyen de beaucoup connaître en voyant peu, de bien voir en observant souvent, de voyager cependant, mais comme on assiste à un spectacle, en laissant les tableaux changeants se renouveler d'eux-mêmes autour d'un point de vue fixe et d'une existence immobile.[4]

One had to travel outside of one's self to experience life. However, for Fromentin the return to oneself and one's own soil was even more important than the trip. For it was within the artistic self that the creative transformation and perception occurred. Only when the experiences of life had been evaluated and their essential meaning crystallized had the artist succeeded in creating something. One must avoid the temptation of passing on raw observation as art.

Thus in *Dominique* the journey is as important a motif as the process of growing up. Arthur Evans[5] suggests that *Dominique* is built on the structure of a circular "voyage," whereas Maija Lehtonen[6] proposes a structure constructed on two concentric circles with Trembles as a kind of axis between them. Both views are interesting and useful. One can see that Dominique's maturing follows his journey away from home as he moves from Trembles through Villeneuve to Ormesson, where he receives his final years of education and awakens to love. From Ormesson he moves to Paris, where he enters the social and intellectual life of the world. From there he goes to Nièvres for the final scene. After his final break with Madeleine (he had abandoned his career in society in the preceding chapter), Dominique quickly withdraws from the world to live a secluded but active life in his own surroundings. Three days after his departure from Nièvres he was with Mme Ceyssac at Ormesson. The next day he resumed his journey ". . . dans cette course lamentable qui me ramenait au gîte comme un animal blessé qui perd du sang et ne veut pas défaillir en route. . . ."[7] The image is apropos. Dominique returns home to his own "lair." It is appropriate that he be welcomed by André, symbol of the de Bray estate, a timeless presence who represents the unchanging permanence and stability of the life which Dominique will now set out to continue.

Lehtonen's suggestion that there is a dual circular structure with Trembles as an axis between the two journeys reminds one that Dominique does indeed return to Trembles from Paris for the summer vacation with Madeleine in chapter 11. The destination and timing of the trip are not without significance. Dominique has been living at Paris in grief since the marriage of Madeleine. When he decides to join her at Trembles, he is returning to his native soil with Madeleine. There she will become associated with the memories and places which form the substance of Dominique's existence. In a sense they return to an innocent time in this setting, one which allows them to resume the friendship which was interrupted by the engagement and marriage. As mentioned above, this journey back to Trembles is an interlude which separates the section concerning the awakening of love and grief from the beginning of the new relationship which will eventually end in permanent separation.

IV *The Seasons*

Given the fact that *Dominique* is a confessional novel in the Romantic tradition, it is not surprising to find a close relationship between nature and the principal character. One of the Romantic aspects of the novel is that Dominique's own personality is seen in close harmony with the seasons. The circular journey mentioned above is paralleled by a seasonal journey. Fromentin is careful to indicate the time of year, weather, and general atmosphere for each scene in the novel. Fromentin had a strong predilection for autumn and mentioned on more than one occasion that he did not like the changeable, unpredictable nature of spring.

It is significant that the entire frame story is set in autumn at harvest time. Both visits of the narrator are at this time of year and find the de Bray estate in peaceful repose following the summer activity. It is a traditional time of celebration and dancing, an opportunity to see the de Bray family in the happy setting which Fromentin intends as a final impression on the reader. However, autumn is also associated with middle age and has a nostalgic tint of the memories of things past. This ambivalence adds to the impression that Dominique's current life is not an unmitigated joy. How much of Dominique's inner spirit participates in his family's serenity and how much is locked in the room of memories and regrets?

It should be noted that the awakening of the love and the emotional turmoil described in chapter 5 take place in the spring. Despite some joyous moments, the basic anxiety, uncertainty, and grief are placed in conjunction with the spring of the year. Madeleine's marriage takes place at the end of winter or in early spring on a frozen day and, in chapter 9, Dominique spends a miserable winter in Paris. Finally, both important episodes with Madeleine take place in autumn. At Trembles, in chapter 11, Dominique says goodbye to the happy summer moments, wishing that he could fix Madeleine's trace forever in the landscape, and the final break with Madeleine at Nièvres occurs in November.

V Symmetry of Characters

In constructing *Dominique* Fromentin sought to create a parallel relationship between Julie and Olivier which could add an additional interest to the novel and which could be used as a kind of mirror image of his own romance in reverse. Just as Dominique is hopelessly in love with Madeleine, so is Julie involved in an impossible love relationship with Olivier. The device is not really successful because the author fails to develop Julie's personality and he does not devote enough time to the development of their affair.

Julie appears very little in the text. She is present in chapter 4 when Dominique meets Madeleine and she is given a prominent role in the wedding scene, as she accompanies Dominique to the ceremony and appears to be as unhappy as he. In chapter 11 Julie plays a significant role in the lighthouse scene. It is she who faints in the arms of Olivier:

Elle était immobile à côté d'Olivier, sa petite main tremblante placée tout près de la main du jeune homme et fortement crispée sur la rampe. . . .[8]

One might interpret these lines as reflecting Julie's fear of the height. But the scene is so clearly symbolic of the emotion aroused by love that the precipice is quite of another sort. Thus one tends to read another meaning into the phrase that "her small, trembling hand was placed near the hand of the young man" and that it was "tightly clenched." In chapter 12 Fromentin focuses on the couple again when Olivier consciously praises Madeleine's beauty in front of Julie and then tells her that she too looks good, although he had not even looked at her. These two rather brief moments are virtually all the preparation given to the scene which undoubtedly accounts for Fromentin's attempt to develop this secondary plot. Olivier asks Dominique to learn whether or not Julie had seen him the other night with another woman. As a background to this, he explains how Julie has loved Olivier since the beginning. Olivier's callous treatment of her precipitates the argument which more or less ends their intimacy. Olivier explains that he has never given Julie the least encouragement and that her stubborn love for him is senseless. Dominique treats Olivier's lack of sympathy for Julie harshly. Exasperated, Olivier makes the comparison which undoubtedly gave rise to the secondary plot:

Je ne l'aime pas, est-ce assez clair? Tu sais ce qu'on entend par aimer ou ne pas aimer; tu sais bien que les deux contraires ont la même énergie, la même impuissance à se gouverner. Essaye donc d'oublier Madeleine; moi, j'essayerai d'adorer Julie; nous verrons lequel de nous deux y réussira le plus tôt.[9]

While it is true that the point is well made and that Julie's love for Olivier is hopeless, it is not true that the situations are really parallel. Dominique's love for Madeleine does not remain unanswered. The obstacle which frustrates him is her marriage. The comparison is good for showing the suffering which accompanies disappointment in love, but the relationship between Olivier and Julie lacks the independent development and interest necessary to balance the love affair of Dominique and Madeleine.

VI *Isolated Moments*

Arthur Evans notes that Fromentin used the same narrative procedure in his novel as he did in the travel books and in *Maîtres d'autrefois*:

Dominique is built up out of a series of relatively isolated scenes and significant moments, each chosen with a discriminating selectivity, brought to a high finish, and presented framed as it were.[10]

The format relates to Fromentin's way of seeing, his tendency to describe a scene in the same orderly fashion and with the same perspective that he used to analyze a painting. But if his painterly eye contributed to the structure of his chapters, so did his memory or the way in which he remembered past events. When he remembered something, even if relatively insignificant, he recalled it in all its detail:

Après des années, le petit espace où j'ai mis ma tente un soir et d'où je suis parti le lendemain m'est présent avec tous ses détails. L'endroit occupé par mon lit, je le vois; il y avait là de l'herbe ou des cailloux, une touffe d'où j'ai vu sortir un lézard, des pierres qui m'empêchaient de dormir.[11]

Dominique likewise stresses the importance of his memory in recalling seemingly unimportant events in great detail, including the precise date and even the day of the week. His is a memory of impressions not of facts:

. . . il se formait en moi je ne sais quelle mémoire spéciale assez peu sensible aux faits, mais d'une aptitude singulière à se pénétrer des impressions.[12]

Ostensibly *Dominique* is a book which recounts the life of Dominique de Bray up to the moment when he returns to Trembles after his separation from Madeleine. Although he begins the narrative with his childhood, how he was raised by Mme Ceyssac and his life under the tutelage of Augustin, Dominique does not attempt to give a chronological account of these years. In fact he merely summarizes the kinds of things he did and learned. Finally, he ends the chapter with the anecdote concerning his essay on Hannibal. The story is not really drawn from an important event in Dominique's life. Rather, his memory of the emotion-filled days which preceded his imminent departure were clustered around this otherwise insignificant incident. The chapters do not really have a chronological focus, even though the narrative constantly moves forward. One is not conscious of time as a factor. What matters in a given season is Dominique's emotional state and the analysis of his feelings through monologues and dialogues.

Dominique spends several years at Ormesson before moving to Paris. In all there are five chapters devoted to his life there. During that time many significant things must have occurred, yet the only real events included in the novel are Madeleine's departure, her marriage, and Dominique's graduation. Obviously, large segments of each chapter are devoted to Dominique's self-analysis and the thoughts passing through his mind. These are nurtured by innumerable, seemingly insignificant moments, a fact which gives the book its static character and creates the impression that the novel lacks plot, incident, and movement.

But the incidents are only insignificant in an objective sense. To Dominique they represent the moments which really crystallized his thoughts or affected him greatly. He recalled his first encounter with Olivier because it came to represent something basic in his nature. When Olivier asks Dominique for the translation of the Latin passage, he reveals an approach to life which is indicative of his character. It is not that he is unable to understand Latin, only that he is unwilling to invest himself in life. He prefers to accept what life will provide, to take the easy pleasure and forego the satisfaction derived from accomplishments which require commitment and effort. In retrospect Dominique remembers the important moment when the flowers from M. de Nièvres arrived. At the time he was unaware of their significance, but later he perceived the relationship between this incident and the change in attitude which he had observed in Madeleine. Throughout the novel he uses quiet moments to mark important changes. The two months he spends with Madeleine at Trembles are focused around two experiences: one is the famous lighthouse scene and the other is their last stroll together. What had seemed to him a timeless period together was suddenly over. Madeleine had experienced with him sites and memories from his past which would remain fixed forever in his memory and which had become a permanent reality which the passage of time could not destroy. Now Madeleine had been made a part of those memories and, as Dominique watches her walk, he wishes that the trace of her footsteps could be retained forever in that place. The recognition that nothing is timeless, even when time seems to stand still, strikes him forcibly. He even recalls the brief comments and the innuendo which accompanied the word *déjà*, which seemed to characterize so well his own thoughts and emotions then and now.

If Fromentin described scenes from the perspective of the painter or art critic, he also framed human settings where the contour of the scene is captured both physically, as if in a group sitting, and verbally. In these moments he brings brief phrases and gestures into the light and holds them there for our examination and gloss. Dominique and the reader must reflect on the real meaning of what was said, while Dominique yet recalls another reflection based on an incident or conversation of great personal significance.

In each chapter Fromentin organizes the material around a few moments which made a great impression on Dominique but are not necessarily important as events. The technique allows him to take advantage of his gift for description of a setting and for the minute analysis of Dominique's reaction to what has happened. Within these isolated moments Fromentin is at his best as an artist. The novel moves away from the objective realism of a chronological narrative toward a series of connected and highly polished scenes in which the action of months can be condensed into a meaningful, dramatic moment.

CHAPTER 8

Know Thyself

I   *Romantic versus Classic*

ALTHOUGH Fromentin was himself a member of the second generation of Romantics, an admirer of Senancour's *Oberman* and Sainte-Beuve's *Volupté*, it is the general consensus that he is repudiating Romanticism and its values in *Dominique*. One can see a number of Romantic traits in Fromentin as well as in his principal character.[1] Young Dominique lives a life of solitude close to nature. He is self-critical and introspective and tends to be haunted by the ideal. Throughout the novel he invests the seasons and nature with emotional overtones of his own personality. In his affair with Madeleine he idealizes their love relationship and even tends to see in her an idealization of his notion of the perfect woman. In his early years he is a perfectionist, is attracted by the Muse, and believes that he has the poetic inspiration characteristic of the genius.

But if Dominique is tempted by the unrealistic dreams of his imagination, the thrust of the novel is against these traits. Far from glorifying individualism, poetic genius, and the *homme fatal*, the book seems to establish the worth of the ordinary man who has found peace in a stable existence close to the soil. Instead of a search for the perfect love in erotic terms, Dominique supports the value of marriage and morality.

The tension between the Romantic and Classic modes can be seen in the form of the novel as well as in the roles of Olivier and Augustin, the two friends who advise Dominique throughout the text. A confessional novel, *Dominique* fits essentially into the Romantic tradition of this form. However, Fromentin was not really comfortable with the Romantic practice of personal confession. By creating a second narrator he eliminated the intimate setting in which the protagonist confides his innermost thoughts and emotions to the reader. Instead one has the more formal, distant setting of a narrator recounting his life to a second party who, although he places the protagonist in direct contact with the reader, is nonetheless present in the frame story to add his commentary and evaluation of the motives and attitudes of the principal narrator. This has the effect of making the account more public and open to rational analysis. In fact, the presence of the anonymous narrator is what characterizes Fromentin's narrative, for Dominique's principal purpose is not to lay bare his heart or to describe the state of his soul, but to examine his thoughts, motives, and actions. As Dominique explains at the end of chapter three, ". . . j'entrai dans la vie sans la haïr, quoiqu'elle m'ait fait beaucoup pâtir, avec un ennemi inséparable, bien intime et positivement mortel: c'était moi-même."[2] It is this critique of the self which forms the substance of the novel rather than the uncritical description of the state and development of his youthful being. During his formative years Dominique recognizes two contradictory tendencies in his own nature. In the novel the two sides of his character are developed in the personalities of his two closest friends, Olivier and Dominique. In a sense the novel is a struggle between these opposite modes of being.

II *Augustin and Olivier*

When one examines the roles of Dominique's two friends, their importance to the structure and meaning of the novel becomes clear. Within the frame story or the part of the text which develops the nature of Dominique's current life, Olivier is introduced first and Augustin last, just the reverse of their introduction in the main narrative. It is important that Olivier be introduced in chapter 2, that is, the Olivier of twenty years later. One does not see the attractive Olivier who had such an influence on Dominique. He sees, instead, a man whose way of life has come to an empty end. At the dinner, near the end of the second chapter, Mme de Bray approaches the subject of marriage in her conversation with Olivier. When he rejects the idea that he should marry, she attacks his basic philosophy by pointing out the selfishness and uselessness of a life that does not serve others in some way. She points out that such a life exists only for itself and its own pleasures. Shortly afterward Olivier returns to his estate where he has been living in total isolation, except for his visits to the de Brays, and attempts suicide. That he should fail becomes important when one hears him explain to Dominique twenty years earlier that his goal was to escape the ennui of life by filling the void with as many pleasures as possible:

Sais-tu quel est mon plus grand souci? c'est de tuer l'ennui. Celui qui rendrait ce service à l'humanité serait le vrai destructeur des monstres. Le vulgaire et l'ennuyeux! toute la mythologie des païens grossiers n'a rien imaginé de plus subtil et de plus effrayant.[3]

His failure to commit suicide is symbolic of his inability to overcome ennui. His disfigurement is likewise symbolic, in that the old Olivier is dead and lives on only in disfigured form. The meaning of the novel hinges on this critique of Olivier twenty years after the fact. Then in the last scene of the book the reader meets Augustin. He is still robust and continues to maintain a close relationship with Dominique.[4]

In the novel proper the two friends play significant roles in chapters 3, 4, 6, 8, 9, 10, and 14. It should be noted that this follows the basic structure discussed in chapter 8. Chapter 3 introduces Augustin as the tutor of Dominique and chapter 4 includes Dominique's first meeting with Olivier as a student at Ormesson. Chapter 6 contrasts Olivier's attitude toward love and the epistolary advice of Augustin. Chapters 8 through 10 develop Dominique's grief after Madeleine's marriage. The two friends present Dominique with opposing ways of dealing with his new life. Chapter 14 provides the resolution of the conflict and neither character has much to do with the novel after that, except for Augustin's appearance at the end.

Augustin's presentation in chapter 3 is lengthy and well developed. Several years older than Dominique, he is brought to Trembles as Dominique's tutor. Because he is older, friendship on an equal basis is not yet possible. But in his capacity as tutor and adviser, he is suitable for the role as Dominique's rational side. Augustin is honest, industrious, and ambitious, quick to act but not without weighing the advantages and disadvantages of his action. Because he has no family, he must make his own way in life and is thus very practical.

Olivier's introduction in chapter 4 is much less extensive. Both boys are in class, each one alone and seeking a friend. Olivier has the appearance and taste of the aristocrat. He scorns the bourgeois and work in general. He is bored with schoolwork and has little interest in reading. However, he was more mature than his years and had an attractive personality. In his first encounter Olivier asks Dominique for a translation of assigned Latin. This sums up the difference between the two friends: Augustin must work to overcome the problems which life presents; Olivier does not engage himself in life and willingly accepts whatever life provides to avoid the bother of dealing with the problem.

In chapters 5 and 6 Dominique goes through the turmoil of awakening love. During Madeleine's absence he spends much time in and around her home reflecting about his feelings. One day Olivier confides in him concerning the affair with Mme X. . . . His bold proposition and detached attitude amaze Dominique. The situation does not seem much related to Dominique's affair, but in reality it is very instructive. As a first romance it parallels Dominique's own experience. Repulsed, Olivier must live with a seemingly hopeless situation. His pride is wounded, but he is determined not to be affected: "Si tu crois que je vais me rendre malheureux, tu te trompes . . .,"[5] he says to Dominique. He plans in his mind how he might some day have the satisfaction of rejecting her. Dominique, who understands little about the affair, can only ask Olivier the ridiculous question: "Es-tu bien sûr de l'aimer?"[6] The question is so lacking in understanding that it stops Olivier for a moment:

Olivier me regarda dans le blanc des yeux, et, comme si ma question lui paraissait le comble de la niaiserie ou de la folie. . . .[7]

The interlude concerning Olivier's romance is over and the text returns to Dominique and Madeleine. Here one sees two different kinds of investment in life. Dominique's question implies the commitment of self which involves risk and possible grief. Olivier has invested nothing of himself but his *amour-propre*. He does not intend to become unhappy whatever the outcome. Once again he remains on the surface of life. When Dominique confides to Olivier the secret that he has begun to write poetry, Olivier is somewhat perplexed but agreeable to the idea: "C'est singulier . . . me dit Olivier; où cela te mènera-t-il? Au fait, tu as raison, si cette occupation t'amuse."[8] In his own way Olivier is as unable to understand this as Dominique was unable to understand his relationship to Mme X. . . . However, it is his conclusion that is important. What Dominique does with his time is of little consequence as long as it amuses him. Throughout his life Olivier will try to fill the void with activities that pass the time amusingly.

The example of Olivier is counteracted by the advice which Dominique finds in Augustin's correspondence. Although it would seem to be of a general nature, since Augustin does not know Dominique's situation and knows Olivier only from Dominique's letters, the advice is really to the point:

La vie n'est facile pour personne, excepté pour ceux qui l'effleurent sans y pénétrer. Pour ceux-là, Paris est le lieu du monde où l'on peut le plus aisément avoir l'air d'exister. Il suffit de se laisser aller dans le courant, comme un nageur dans une eau lourde et rapide. On y flotte et l'on ne s'y noie pas.[9]

The passage ostensibly refers to his own situation and Dominique's, but the image of floating on the surface of the water applies to Olivier and his approach to life. The same is true for his comment on ennui, a response to Dominique's own lament: "l'ennui n'est fait que pour les esprits vides et pour les coeurs qui ne sauraient être blessés de rien. . . ."[10] Olivier refuses the kind of emotional involvement which makes one vulnerable to personal loss. The result is a meaningless, empty existence.

After the wedding Augustin, who is not supposed to know the cause of Dominique's grief and ennui (we learn later that he had guessed), counsels Dominique that life is the remedy for all things:

La vie, croyez-moi, voilà la grande antithèse et le grand remède à toutes les souffrances dont le principe est une erreur. Le jour où vous mettrez le pied dans la vie, dans la vie réelle, entendez-vous bien; le jour où vous la connaîtrez avec ses lois, ses nécessités, ses rigueurs, ses devoirs et ses chaînes, ses difficultés et ses peines, ses vraies douleurs et ses enchantements, vous verrez comme elle est saine, et belle, et forte, et féconde, en vertu même de ses exactitudes. . . .[11]

Augustin's advice to enter life resembles, on the surface at least, the advice given by Olivier in chapter 9. He outlines the impasse that Dominique has reached: he loves Madeleine, but she cannot be his. He must emerge from this impasse. Dominique must recognize that Madeleine is not the only woman in the world. Had fate wished it, he could have just as easily fallen in love with another. Olivier does not say to forget Madeleine only to replace her with another:

Ce que je veux . . . c'est que tu sortes de ta tanière, esprit chagrin, pauvre coeur blessé. Tu t'imagines que la terre a pris le deuil et que la beauté s'est voilée, et que tous les visages sont en larmes, et qu'il n'y a plus ni espérances, ni joies, ni voeux comblés, parce que dans ce moment la destinée te maltraite. Regarde donc un peu autour de toi, et mêle-toi à la foule des gens qui sont heureux ou qui croient l'être.[12]

Immediately after Olivier's long discourse and his invitation that Dominique join him at the theater, Augustin enters. When Dominique tells him that he has burned all his poetry, Augustin responds in a way which characterizes his approach to existence: "C'est à recommencer, dit-il sans s'émouvoir autrement; je connais cela."[13]

Both men urge Dominique to participate in life. Olivier sees life as a deadly tedium which man must never aid in its effort to kill him. One must escape the boredom of existence by partaking of the pleasures which life offers. Augustin's view of life is also sober. As he tells Dominique in chapter 10, the question is not to know whether or not one is happy ". . . mais de savoir si l'on a tout fait pour le devenir."[14] But he believes in the ultimate worth of existence and that life pays rewards to those who invest themselves and make the effort. Both men ask Dominique to replace Madeleine but in very different manners. Olivier treats the relationship as a light infatuation which can be replaced by seeking another. When he says *remplacer* he means displace her in your life. Augustin would have Dominique replace Madeleine in another way. He would have him turn his attention to living, to other activities of interest which will gradually fill the void left by his loss. At the end of chapter 10, Dominique attempts to follow Olivier's advice by taking a mistress. After two months he recognizes that this meaningless pretense has led nowhere. In chapter 14 Olivier and Dominique reach a crossroad. While they remain friends, they nonetheless have a parting of the ways. As Fromentin writes, it marked the end of their intimate relationship. It is the point when Dominique abandons his so-called Romantic side in favor of reason.

III *Know Thyself*

In final analysis the repudiation of the values of Romanticism and the rivalry between Augustin and Olivier serve to point up the real meaning of the novel. On the last page of the book the narrator makes his final evaluation of Dominique: ". . . un esprit dont la plus réelle originalité était d'avoir strictement suivi la maxime ancienne de se connaître soi-même . . . ."[15] *Dominique* is a confessional novel in which the author is less interested in describing the *état d'âme* of the protagonist than in analyzing how he arrived at an understanding of himself and life. Throughout the book he describes how Dominique came to see himself objectively, as he really was and not as he fancied himself or hoped to be.

To many the assessment he makes of his own worth and life in the opening chapter seems harsh and is seen as the tacit reflection of the protagonist's failure in the novel:

Certainement je n'ai pas à me plaindre . . . car, Dieu merci, je ne suis plus rien, à supposer que j'aie jamais été quelque chose, et je souhaite à beaucoup d'ambitieux de finir ainsi. J'ai trouvé la certitude et le repos, ce qui vaut mieux que toutes les hypothèses. Je me suis mis d'accord avec moi-même, ce qui est bien la plus grande victoire que nous puissions remporter sur l'impossible. Enfin, d'inutile à tous, je deviens utile à quelques-uns, et j'ai tiré de ma vie, qui ne pouvait rien donner de ce qu'on espérait d'elle, le seul acte peut-être qu'on n'en attendît pas, un acte de modestie, de prudence et de raison. Je n'ai donc pas à me plaindre. Ma vie est faite et bien faite selon mes désirs et mes mérites.[16]

It is the kind of statement a disappointed man makes who is making the best of his disillusionment. Somehow the scenes of familial love and his own statements concerning his contentment and pleasure at working with the land and being useful to others do not entirely erase the gnawing regret of his past life represented by his room of memories. In part this is the feeling which the author intended to convey. But to see Dominique's life as a failure is to take his life out of context. Ironically enough it is Olivier's perspective of happiness and life which provides the context in which Dominique's statements must be understood:

Le bonheur, le vrai bonheur, est un mot de légende. Le paradis de ce monde s'est refermé sur les pas de nos premiers parents; voilà quarante-cinq mille ans qu'on se contente ici-bas de demi-perfections, de demi-bonheurs et de demi-moyens.[17]

To seek pure happiness is to dream the impossible, to fail to deal with life in a realistic way. To succeed is to recognize that one must be content with the *demi-bonheurs* which life provides. Again Augustin's life is the example of a successful existence. Not that he is the ideal individual, but he has made the best of what life has given him. When Dominique concludes that his poetry merited the obscurity it received, that his political writings, although they enjoyed a certain renown, were, nonetheless, of no lasting worth, he is being honest about their quality in an absolute sense. To spend his life in pursuit of making a contribution where he lacks the talent would be a waste and would bring grief in the end. At one time he felt himself inspired by the Muse, but when he found that all he had felt was not new, that he was not unique, he recognized that any pretense to poetic genius would only be a parody of the truly gifted poets. The acceptance of one's limited talents takes more courage than the more customary escape into one's fantasies and aspirations. It is easier to live in the glory of success and to believe that one's renown is merited than to admit that one's fame has little to do with the substance of one's work. Dominique has found all the happiness that life permitted him to have. He does not pretend to have had nothing but happiness and success. Nor does he pretend that he has forgotten his unhappy love affair or that it no longer causes him any pain. However, given his limitations and those of life itself, he has managed to find peace and happiness.

Some seem to look upon Dominique's current life as if it were static and held no future possibilities of development. His own view is quite the reverse and gives a quietly optimistic tone to the future for himself and his son:

Si j'avais été ce que je ne suis pas, j'estimerais que la famille des de Bray a assez produit, que sa tâche est faite, et que mon fils n'a plus qu'à se reposer; mais la Providence en a décidé autrement, les rôles sont changés. Est-ce tant mieux ou tant pis pour lui? Je lui laisse l'ébauche d'une vie inachevé, qu'il accomplira, si je ne me trompe. Rien ne finit, reprit-il, tout se transmet, même les ambitions.[18]

His son's life is just beginning. He undoubtedly will have the aspirations of youth and may even accomplish things which Dominique was unable to do. Dominique does not look upon his own life as finished, only fixed in the path he has chosen to follow. If one recalls Fromentin's aesthetic values, he sees that the truly creative part of Dominique's life is taking place. He has found his way and is in the process of perfecting it.

Today it is difficult to accept the conclusion of *Dominique* in optimistic terms. Post-eighteenth-century man does not accept the essential philosophical premise that postlapsarian reality can only be imperfect nor that man's nature is divided between reason and the senses and that his reason must control the senses if he is to be a balanced, civilized human being. Dominique's idea of a happy life is one in which the soul is at peace with itself and the individual enjoys a harmonious relationship with society. The modern world tends to see man in conflict with the social order. Reason is associated with the strictures of a hostile society and man's freedom is identified with the unfettered subconscious and a liberation of the senses. It is only natural that Dominique's deliberate renunciation of the part of himself represented by Olivier should strike some as a failure. To them he fails to accept the challenge of life to probe the unknown, to explore the possibilities of existence. For Fromentin such a perspective represents a formless wandering through the raw materials of art without recognizing that one is only experiencing numberless repetitions in various shapes of what one has already seen. It is to make the error of emphasizing subject over form, of mistaking novelty for art.

CHAPTER 9

Characters and Psychology

I *Minor Characters*

*D*OMINIQUE has frequently been criticized for its lack of action and movement. In his general appraisal of Fromentin shortly after the author's death, Emile Montégut had harsh words for the work and Fromentin's conception of it: "Il crut, selon toute apparence, qu'il se tirerait d'affaire avec des descriptions et de la psychologie."[1] Although Montégut himself felt that Fromentin's characters were *sans relief* ("without dimension"), he recognized the quality of minute analysis that went into the work. In the introduction to her critical edition, Barbara Wright laments that Fromentin, in an effort to make the contrast between Augustin and Olivier more pronounced, initiated changes in the text which made both characters less interesting as human beings and more like cardboard figures with only one-dimensional personalities.[2] The criticism pertains basically to the secondary personages, of course, and not to the principal character.

Part of the difficulty lies in the use of a first-person narrator who has the disadvantage of knowing only what he perceives of the other characters. The secondary narrator might have added another perspective and other information, but Fromentin really makes very little use of him, except for a few comments about Dominique himself. Not given the opportunity to know the other characters personally, he is unable to comment on them independently. The reader and the narrator know only as much as Dominique tells them.

A second factor in the weakness of the other characters is the intense focus of the book on the relationship between Dominique and Madeleine. Fromentin could have broadened the roles of the secondary characters and given their lives an independent interest or had them play a larger role in forming the reader's opinion concerning the love relationship between Dominique and Madeleine. However, they are limited to the incidental role which Dominique gives them.

Beyond this one must say that there is very little development of anyone's personality in the manner of the classic nineteenth-century novel. Fromentin scarcely explores the intellectual interests or personal tastes of his characters. Rather he uses a traditional psychology which examines personal reactions to the moral issues of the text. Fromentin's aesthetic values drew him away from the individualization which became so prominent in post-eighteenth-century thought. One can see this in his travel literature. He was not interested in portraying the anecdote and peculiar details which characterized the North African Arab, but rather sought to capture the essential quality of North Africa and the people by eliminating what he considered superficial detail. The same motivation caused him to look within his characters to seek the central axis of their moral natures.

Even if one grants this premise, Fromentin's character presentation strikes one as too prescriptive. He does not allow his characters the freedom of individual action. Instead of allowing his characters to reveal themselves through their actions, he has Dominique simply describe their natures to the reader. One is told that Mme Ceyssac is serious and pious. She followed the laws of church and state and loved *des choses surannés* ("old-fashioned things"). The only actions which allow her to demonstrate this character are her pleasure in learning that Olivier is from a respected noble family and her reception of Dominique when he is returning to Trembles after his final separation from Madeleine. Madame de Bray is treated in a similar way. The narrator portrays her as an attractive woman and an excellent mother and wife. She has a kind nature, is gracious, has a good head for figures, and is adept at managing the estate. Her presence is important for what it says about Dominique's current life. It helps to answer the question concerning his failure or success and does not really focus on her as a character in her own right. Only her scene with Olivier permits the reader to evaluate her by her actions. She argues for marriage as a means of making one's existence worthwhile, in that it makes one's life useful to others. One might accuse her here of a certain insensitivity in treating Olivier so harshly. However, this is not really her intent. One is not focusing on her personality. Her role in the scene is to bring out the ideas which the author considers vital to the text's meaning. As such she is not really in conflict with Olivier personally. The important thing is that he will react to the ideas which provoke a crisis in his own life.

Perhaps the least satisfactory character is Julie. Dominique scarcely tells us enough about her to give any indication of her nature. This was probably his intent. It is clear that she was an enigma to Dominique, as he refers to her as being sphinx-like. One learns that she loves Olivier, is easily hurt by his indifference to her, and that she is disturbed when Madeleine is married. But one has no idea what she is like and Dominique does not seem to know what she thinks or feels about Olivier beyond his belief that she loves him. The impossible romance between Julie and Oliver does not serve well as a balance or parallel for the main story. Julie's own personality and personal struggle require more attention and development. Her participation is too limited for her unrequited love to serve as an effective counterpart to the relationship between Dominique and Madeleine.

II *Augustin and Olivier*

Because of the contrast he wishes to make, Fromentin gives a much more detailed analysis of the characters of Augustin and Olivier. In chapter 3 Dominique makes an extensive summary of Augustin's personal qualities. The reader is told that Augustin is the epitome of honesty, courage, and kindness. He has excellent judgment, is modest, has lofty ideals, a strong will, and an infectious enthusiasm for life and his future despite personal difficulties. His lack of financial security forces him to have a practical turn of mind and even to be very ambitious.[3] Dominique informs us that Augustin is well educated and that his learning is reflected in his judgment and wisdom.

Yet Augustin is not filled out as a character; he remains one-dimensional. Augustin's part is so dominated by his role as tutor that one does not see him much in other capacities. Dominique reads from some of the letters which Augustin wrote to him after their years at Trembles. The letters are full of advice urging Dominique to be diligent in his work and to live in reality. He warns him against the pitfalls of ennui and gently suggests the potential weaknesses in Olivier's character so as to alert him to the dangers there. But there is very little in these letters or in the future visit of Dominique to Augustin's home which gives a better idea of Augustin's personality. The reader knows that he attempted to write for the theater and then turned to journalism. To Dominique's eyes the life he lives is meager, although Augustin's wife seems happy enough and is confident that the future will satisfy her needs. The image of the life Augustin leads confirms our idea of a hard-working, worthy man whose will and tenacity may earn him a modest success. Yet one would like to know something of the kind of theater he tried to write and perhaps something about his dealings with the theatrical and journalistic worlds. One does not even know what Augustin thinks of his wife or his domestic life. Seeing him in various situations or in discussions of subjects which interested him might have helped to give a more rounded picture of Augustin.

One's only glimpse of an Augustin not in the tutor's role comes from almost insignificant items. When Dominique and Augustin separate at Ormesson, it is Augustin who shows the greater emotion and affection. Moreover, his genuine interest in Dominique is reflected in his continued correspondence and effort to be of help. He is willing to take the time to become acquainted with Madeleine, despite the pressures of his own busy life. One also sees a sensitive side to the practical Augustin. He early perceives the youth's love for Madeleine. yet he is careful not to pry or to give any hint that he knows what lies behind the ennui and general disquietude reflected in Dominique's letters. And although he always uses phrases which indicate the difference in their ages, he is sensitive enough to vary the tone of his letters as Dominique grows older to make their dialogue more of a discourse between mature adults.

Olivier's judgment of Augustin is harsh and reflects his own attitude toward life:

Il y aura toujours chez lui du précepteur et du parvenu. Il sera pédant et en sueur, comme tous les gens qui n'ont pour eux que le vouloir et qui n'arrivent que par le travail. J'aime mieux des dons d'esprit ou de la naissance, ou faute de cela, j'aime mieux rien.[4]

Dominique himself called Augustin *une nature incomplète* (p. 54), obviously referring to the lack of a more spiritual side to his character. However, in changes he made to the manuscript, Fromentin diminished Dominique's personal aversion for his tutor. He did not wish to weaken Augustin's position opposite Olivier. Thus he removed the statement that Dominique himself had trouble liking Augustin. Professor Wright correctly points out that Fromentin did a disservice to the book in removing Dominique's own ambivalence for

Augustin. It lessens the conflict within Dominique and reduces a side of his character which is already weak.

The character of Olivier seems drawn from the classic Romantic figure and has many traits which remind one of Werther, René, Amaury, or Oberman. Dominique describes him as a handsome, somewhat delicate, blond individual who has the air of an aristocratic dandy, except that he has none of the taste for art or the artificial. Olivier loves the pleasures and grand life of Paris and he takes great care in his attire, although he does not continually attend to himself once he is dressed. Those who meet him invariably find him charming and attractive. He learns easily, although he reads little, and he finds Latin and literature boring. Questioning the use of it, Olivier scorns those who write books. He is so irregular in his habits and so undisciplined that he himself has no interest in study. At one time he traveled much, but he soon grew weary of it and returned to his provincial estate to live alone and withdrawn from society. Even as a young man he was morose, filled with self-disgust, and gave the impression of being indifferent and blasé. Like his earlier Romantic counterparts, he was young and yet felt old at the same time.

Dominique notes that Olivier was his inferior in much that pertained to the intellect and that he was not nearly so advanced in his studies. Yet in mundane matters it is Olivier who is much more aware of the ways of the world. While Dominique is groping to understand his own feelings and is just beginning to realize that Madeleine has reached another stage in the process of maturing, Olivier already knows that Madeleine has reached a marriageable age. Dominique is unaware of the significance of the bouquet of flowers, whereas Olivier quickly seizes the attached card to take note of the sender's name. Dominique is only gradually awakening to the meaning of his strange feelings for Madeleine, while Olivier has already made advances to a married woman. In such matters Olivier is precocious. He understands the significance of Dominique's emotions well before Dominique himself perceives what they mean. In fact he sees so clearly into the situation that he outlines the scenario for the love affair between Dominique and Madeleine long before it occurs.

In his description of Olivier's character the author observes that he is an *aimable garçon* and that he has an attractive personality. When one analyzes his role in the text, however, there are few instances when this side of his character is revealed. Perhaps the only incident that shows the friendship which Olivier feels for Dominique occurs in chapter 6 when Dominique has entered Madeleine's room during her absence from Ormesson. Olivier returns before Dominique can exit and undoubtedly understands the reason for his presence. Olivier is sensitive to Dominique's plight and makes no reference to his presence there. Aside from this occasion one sees little evidence of the expression of intimacy and close friendship which would improve Olivier's role in the text.[5]

As Olivier appears in the final version of the novel, only his selfishness and rather cruel disregard for others is apparent. Although one can sympathize with him for being exasperated by Julie's unwelcome affection, it is not easy to overlook his callous disregard for her feelings and his deliberate cruelty during the ball scene. The same insolent attitude is evident when he hears that Dominique has been touched by Augustin's plight. Olivier refuses to commit himself to any sincere relationship and his reaction to those who do is the cynical laughter of one who would pretend that anyone who can believe that values must undergird such relationships is naive. It is the source of his ennui and leads him to seek an escape from his own self disgust in the superficial pleasures offered by Parisian society. Unfortunately, Fromentin emphasizes this side of Olivier's character and does not develop a sincere side to his personality.

III *Madeleine and Dominique*

Of all the major characters one probably knows least about Madeleine. She suffers more than others from being seen only through Dominique's eyes. It is ironic, because Dominique watches her more closely and analyzes her every look and word with care. It is as if his great love for her hinders his ability to know her. Both Augustin and Olivier are quoted more extensively. Direct quotations from Madeleine are generally brief and in response to Dominique. One often sees her react to Dominique's words and actions, but the meaning of her reactions is rarely clear and the interpretation of them by Dominique is open to question.

The introductory portrait of Madeleine reveals less about her character than her dress. Dominique stresses her upbringing in a convent and describes her dreary clothing as a reflection of this background. One only learns that she has the shyness and awkwardness of someone raised away from society and that she is deemed pretty.

Critics often write that Dominique idealizes Madeleine, that he creates in his mind the image of a woman different from the reality. This parallels what is generally thought to have been the case in real life between Fromentin and Jenny. The few comments one has from those who knew her describe Jenny in unflattering terms as a coquette and as someone not really worthy of Fromentin's serious attention. This does not accord with the respectful tone and adoration of Fromentin's own attitude. There is, of course, no justification for interpreting the fictional romance as a mere copy of the author's personal experience. But if one analyzes the bits and pieces of dialogue and Madeleine's reactions apart from Dominique's interpretation of them, one finds that Madeleine's personality varies under stress and, at times, seems contradictory.

When Madeleine returns from her trip with her father, she appears changed, more mature to Dominique. At the awards ceremony and at the ball in chapter 12, Madeleine appears to be a person who enjoys society and the social life of Paris. She looks forward to the event, though she tells Dominique that it will be as much pain for her as for him, and during the evening she is described more than once as enjoying herself. This attitude accords with a few scenes in which she appears coquettish and provocative, but it contrasts sharply with the picture of suffering and courage seen throughout the text.

At Trembles, toward the end of their vacation, Madeleine surprises Dominique in the park and teases him about writing a sonnet. Dominique does not realize that Olivier has told her of his writing. He asks if she thinks him capable of writing poetry. She answers that he is capable of doing that. When he protests that Olivier should not have told her, she replies:

Il a bien fait de m'avertir; sans lui, je vous aurais cru une passion malheureuse, et je sais maintenant ce qui vous distrait: ce sont des rimes.[6]

Dominique stresses that she emphasized the word *rimes* in teasing him. Against the background of the preceding scene in which she seemed to become aware that Dominique loves her, one might see this as relief on her part that she was wrong. However, as much as she tries to avoid a situation in which he could declare his love, she seems, at times, to assume his love and to use the knowledge coquettishly. At the ball in chapter 12, Madeleine approaches the gloomy Dominique to inquire whether or not he intends to dance. When he answers negatively, she reproaches him: "Pas même avec moi?" One could take this as the remark of a friend, but it could be seen as the language of flirtation.

These moments of possible flirtation are in harmony with Madeleine's character in chapter 17, when Dominique sees her for the first time after a two-year absence. Unexplainably she momentarily assumes the role of a seductive, even provocative, woman in the famous scene where she insists that Dominique mount her husband's horse and accompany her on a wild ride into the country. Dominique must chase after her in fits and starts. Finally he catches up to her and insists that she stop this cruel game or he would commit suicide. She looks him straight in the eye and then returns calmly to the chateau and goes to her room. Given the nature of the ride and Madeleine's actions, one might well question whether or not Madeleine expected a different reaction from Dominique. Finally, just before the scene with the shawl, it appears as though Madeleine were looking for Dominique. How innocent is she in falling into his arms?

But this side of Madeleine, if one can even call it that, is scarcely visible when one considers the text as a whole. For the most part one sees Madeleine suffering silently, caught between friendship and a growing recognition of love. Although one sees her in a number of scenes where she is under attack from Dominique, who would like to force her to admit she loves him, not so much is learned about her character as one would hope. Just as the heroine in *La Princess de Clèves*, Madeleine must invent various means of avoiding a discussion that could permit Dominique to declare his love. For a while she answers ingenuously, as if she does not understand the innuendo or implication of Dominique's remarks. However, Fromentin does not recreate the situations but merely has Dominique report her strategy. This prevents a certain revelation of Madeleine's personality. Another means Madeleine uses is silence and the deflection of the conversation by a change of subject. And, finally, when Dominique refuses to be put off, she sits silently in grief and despair. Because her defense must be one of silence the opportunity for character analysis in these crucial situations is slight.

The minute analysis of Dominique's thoughts and emotions as he develops from adolescence to maturity remains within a classic framework. Although one sees him as a mature man and, through his own eyes, over a considerable span of time during his youth, one knows somewhat less than one might expect about his worldly interests and activities. Fromentin presents, rather, the classic struggle between Dominique's emotions and reason. The obstacle which prevents Dominique's love for Madeleine from coming to fruition represents the realities of life which often stand in the way of one's complete happiness. Fromentin sees the process of maturing and finding happiness in the ability to adjust one's sights and emotions to the realities of life. He does not see unmitigated joy as part of reality. If one is to find a measure of happiness in life, he must develop the possible pleasures and minimize the inevitable griefs. He who can come to accept reality and concentrate on the positive qualities of his existence can overcome the feeling that he has failed merely because he has not fulfilled all his dreams.

When one analyzes the opening statement by Dominique (as quoted by the narrator), one sees that he assesses his life in just this way. Dominique affirms that he is content with his lot and happy to have no longer the ambitions and desires which caused him so much grief. However, the initial statement is cast in such negative terms that one doubts the contentedness he claims.[7] One wonders whether his subsequent statement is not that of someone trying to persuade himself that he is happy.

In the frame story Dominique is presented as having reached his goal. Although he was very different by nature from those with whom he lived, he nonetheless had become half peasant, he tells us, by being brought up among them. It is this side of his nature which is now being served and is content. He loves the things of the soil, enjoys living a useful life among the people he has known for so long, and loves his family.[8] When he discusses his writings and public life, he acknowledges that he had gained some fame. But, he points out, he assessed his work objectively and decided that it was not worthy of lasting attention. Any fame he received from it would be the false notoriety of superficial success and not related to the real worth of his work.

Within his contentment, however, there is regret: the regret for Paris, the nostalgic memories associated with his room, his preference for autumn as a season, his insistence on hunting alone, and his desire not to have the old days recalled by Père Jacques. It is the tension between regret and contentment in the frame story which makes the main narrative of such interest. Fromentin does not use the third-person narrative, as if the story had an objective reality.

Rather, he has Dominique retell his own tale; he has him rethink the events, words, and gestures aloud just as he has done hundreds of times to himself. This allows one the vividness of reality as it is happening and also permits one to assess the emotional impact of the events on the narrator.

Dominique's analysis of the events really involves his own development as a human being from the young boy growing up among the peasants and his own private thoughts to the chagrined adult who deliberately returns to the peasants to make the best of life. In the process Dominique focuses on a few important periods of development. The picture of Dominique's carefree youth is concluded by the essay on Hannibal's departure. Dominique's own emotional response to the text represents his own feeling about leaving Trembles and entering the world. At Ormesson he is introduced to love. But the importance of Fromentin's psychological analysis is not in describing his conduct once in love, it is rather the portrayal of gradual recognition. Fromentin's analysis follows the process as slowly as if one were watching the physical growth of the adolescent. He moves from the desire to be alone through several incidents with Madeleine that, aided by comments from Olivier, eventually open his eyes to something which, to him, did not exist before. Once Dominique is aware of his love, he is slow to relate its importance to life and reality. This delay and the importance of one year at this moment in life are as fatal to his happiness as the Duc de Nemours's absence from Paris at the moment when Mlle de Chartres becomes available for marriage. When Dominique finally realizes that Madeleine is to be married, the shock is similar to his recognition of love. It had been there for some time; he simply could not perceive it until now. Fromentin carefully portrays the subsequent grief mixed with confusion. It is no wonder that Augustin reenters the text at this point. For the first time in his life, Dominique's reason must play a significant role. It must assess the situation and try to piece together a future suddenly shattered by reality.

While he listens to the counsel of Olivier and Augustin, another development is taking place within him. He is becoming a man, a fact which plays a major part in his treatment of Madeleine. From the moment he steps down from the platform at the awards ceremony, he discards a schoolboy's robes for a man's place in society. Fromentin subtly follows his development from the timid boy who is content to be near Madeleine to the sensual man who attempts to force

Madeleine to confess her love. Despite the grief he causes her and his repeated repentance because of it, he returns to take pleasure in conversations and situations which end in Madeleine's grief and silence. In chapter 17 he gloats about his feeling of power over Madeleine, that she is finally in his power. After two years of public involvement, he returns for his final victory. But throughout this growth, there is within him the human feeling that causes him to repent of the misery he causes her. Dominique sees his own development in these terms, as a beast which lets its adversary loose instinctively:

J'ai honte de vous le dire, ce cri de véritable agonie réveilla en moi le seul instinct qui me restât d'un homme, la pitié. . . . Je n'ai pas à me vanter d'un acte de générosité qui fut presque involontaire, tant la vraie conscience humaine y eut peu de part! Je lâchai prise comme une bête aurait cessé de mordre.[9]

The fully mature adult who had begun the process of rational assessment in chapter 16 now returns to Trembles to begin an existence controlled by reason rather than his senses. No longer will he try to live for his own pleasures and satisfaction. He will guide his life into a useful path which is compatible with his ability and with reality.

CHAPTER 10

Setting, Symbols, and Silence

I *Season and Setting*

EVEN a cursory reading of Fromentin's *Lettres de Jeunesse* and hi two travel accounts makes one aware that the painter and novelis was sensitive to the seasons of the year and nature. Given the solitary nature of his youth and the pleasure he found when at St. Maurice, i is no wonder that he identified his moods with the seasons and nature. In his travel accounts Fromentin never forgets that man must be the center of attention in great art and that his goal is not a description of the North African countryside or its villages. However, Fromentin saw a close relationship between the setting and those who live in it. In analyzing and characterizing the desert during its rainy season and great drought, he learned something about the inhabitants whose lives must, to some extent, be governed by the radical changes of climate and the nature of the landscape. Their temperament and nature must be related to the character of the desert in some way.

In *Dominique* Fromentin naturally wove into the thread of the narrative a close connection between Dominique's own personality and the seasons and natural settings of the text. This is evident from the beginning in the frame story when Dominique, a character self-described as having a natural penchant for regrets and melancholy, is associated with autumn, a time of year when one can look back on the golden days of summer with some regret yet enjoy the peaceful, secure fruits of the harvest after the work and turmoil of the summer have been completed. It is appropriate that Dominique, now past forty years of age, married and fixed in his goals, should retell his story in the autumn of the year. It is a story which seeks to find a balance between the element of regret and the joyous, peaceful setting of the family estate amid the customary festive celebration occasioned by the harvest. Thus in chapter 1 autumn provides a suitable atmosphere for the almost daily hunting expeditions which Dominique insists on taking alone. The implication is that company would interrupt his thoughts, thereby diminishing the moments when the private man can live apart from the public. Likewise the even temperature and consistent weather make an excellent background for the family greeting and celebrations of chapters 1 and 2.

For Fromentin autumn, permanence, and perfection are related. It is a time of year when the lack of turbulence lends a timeless quality to the moment, neither increasing in heat nor yet giving indication of the future change in season, as if winter were not just weeks away. This "eternal" quality is emphasized in chapter 2 when the narrator returns at the exact time of year to find everything unchanged, even the musician:

Les vendanges se firent et s'achevèrent comme les précédentes, accompagnées des mêmes danses, des mêmes festins, au son de la même cornemuse maniée par le même musicien.[1]

Fromentin's emphasis on the repetition of the event, just as André and Père Jacques live on as if permanent fixtures from one generation to the next, adds to the timelessness of the setting. It is as though winter, summer, and spring had not intervened or had not altered the situation; the passage of time and the inevitable process of change which it brings are eliminated by reliving the same moment together.

In the same way Dominique preserves the continuity of self through his memory, the recollection of past events preserved in the symbolic inner chamber. When we return to the present and the frame story in chapter 18 at the end of Dominique's reminiscence we are still in autumn. We have moved from one autumn to the next, separated by more than twenty years, from the autumn of regret to the autumn which represents the mixed existence of the middle-aged man. The narrative began in the quiet of the mind at midday. When the narrative closes, the shadows are beginning to cover the visible signs on the walls which hold the secret to the past:

Le jour baissait à mesure que la paix des souvenirs s'établissait aussi sur son visage. L'ombre envahissait l'intérieur poudreux et étouffé de la petite chambre où se terminait cette longue série d'évocations dont plus d'une avait été douloureuse. Des inscriptions des murailles, on ne distinguait presque plus rien. L'image extérieure et l'image intérieure palissaient donc en même temps, comme si tout ce passé ressuscité par hasard rentrait à la même minute, et pour n'en plus sortir, dans le vague effacement du soir et de l'oubli.[2]

Sounds from the activity outside break the silence. Dominique and the narrator return to the present reality. It is not clear whether the purgative experience of the day is to be conclusive or only an example of how the past still lives, a kind of timeless present in Dominique's inner being. The ambiguity of the scene remains, just as the balance between Dominique's satisfaction and regret is yet in doubt.

Within the narrative proper, the important moments of happiness are associated with autumn as well. During the interlude at Trembles when Dominique and Madeleine enjoy two uninterrupted months of bliss together, the season is once more autumn. Again there is a kind of joining of past and present. Although Madeleine has been married for some time, the couple virtually returns to their earlier companionship prior to the engagement. In seeing Trembles Madeleine comments to Dominique: "Votre pays vous ressemble . . ." ("Your country resembles you . . . ," p. 171). It is as if this return to Dominique's source allows him to associate Madeleine with his true self, a joining of their natures in a union of permanence. This is reinforced by Fromentin's use of image and setting, two traits studied later in the chapter.

During two months they were frequently on board a fishing boat when the weather was *particulièrement calme et beau* ("particularly calm and beautiful," p. 177). They sailed on *une mer lourde, plate et blanche au soleil comme de l'étain* ("a heavy sea, smooth and white in the sun like tin," p. 177). The fisherman drew in his nets hour after hour only to return everything to the sea and the boat continued *à la dérive*, while they watched the sea or the land appear to rise and fall or measured "l'ombre du soleil qui tournait autour du mât comme autour de la longue aiguille d'un cadran, affaiblis par la pesanteur du jour, par le silence, éblouis de lumière, privés de conscience et pour ainsi dire frappés d'oubli par ce long bercement sur des eaux calmes."[3] Although the boat is in perpetual movement and the fisherman constantly brings up new things from the deep, the permanence of the moment is not broken.[4] Just as days bring superficial events so does the fisherman bring new and strange life from the sea, but these pass back into the sea and the essence of the day remains unchanged as the sun revolves in circular fashion around the mast of the boat. Dominique recognized these days as the most peaceful and yet dangerous of his life, just as the tower-chamber represents moments of peace and danger. As he looks at Madeleine he sees the timeless moment of their relationship fixed in her slumber: "Madeleine, à demi couchée, dormait. Ses mains molles et légèrement ouvertes s'étaient séparées de celles du comte."[5] The afternoon of calm on the sea, later a symbol of passion and the temptation of love, represents the summer interlude, itself an illusion of a timeless period when the two lovers are together. For this moment Madeleine's hands are not joined to the count's. Even her sleep may serve to indicate Madeleine's own unawareness of the significant separation which Dominique alone perceives, for Julie's attention is elsewhere. Fromentin's use of season, setting, and imagery is at times extraordinary and lends depth to the novel.

Fromentin uses spring and the weather less extensively as settings. His well-known hostility toward spring is expressed in a letter to Emile Beltrémieux, 4 May 1847:

L'automne a je ne sais quoi de grave et de magnifique qui prête aux lieux les plus ingrats un charme extraordinaire, le charme du regret, la réverbération sereine du soleil qui s'en va; le printemps laisse à toute chose sa plate, son indigente réalité.[6]

In spring is the inconstancy, the changeable, banal reality which characterizes daily life within the temporal setting. Spring is used as a setting for the disturbing awakening of love while a student at Ormesson. Fromentin stresses the restlessness of Dominique, his need to be on the move. All about him there are *insectes nouveau-nés* ("newly born insects," p. 86), flowers blooming, children flying kites, sick people convalescing, a veritable *puberté printanière* ("spring puberty," p. 86) filled the atmosphere.

When the summer and autumn have passed, Dominique notes a change in Madeleine:

. . . je crus apercevoir sur le visage de Madeleine une ombre et comme un souci qui n'y avait jamais paru. Sa cordialité, toujours égale, contenait autant d'affection, mais plus de gravité. Une appréhension, un regret peut-être, quelque chose dont l'effet seul était visible venait de s'introduire entre nous comme un premier avis de désunion.[7]

Dominique notes that *l'hiver approchait*, the winter preceding the turbulent spring which would follow Madeleine's marriage, an event which took place on a day in late winter *par une gelée rigoureuse* ("during a severe frost," p. 126, Wright). The bleakness of reality as it forcibly invaded Dominique's dream reminds one that Olivier departed from Dominique's home in late autumn, after the important conversation about marriage with Mme de Bray, on a night described as *clair et froide* ("clear and cold," p. 45). The discussion had seriously called into question the value of Olivier's life. It forced him to argue not only that his own selfishness put marriage out of the question but even that consideration of others did not allow him to inflict himself upon anyone. On the night that Olivier returns to his estate, it is as clear and cold out as his own mind is lucid and isolated. Fromentin has set the tone for his forthcoming attempted suicide.

As in the boat scene discussed above, Fromentin often provides a physical setting which reinforces the atmosphere set in the climate and season. In the turbulent, passionate moments after they have climbed to the top of the lighthouse, Fromentin emphasizes the swaying structure, high winds, the fragility of the railing, the frightening height, and the violence of the sea and rocks below. The dizzying, terrifying experience has them transfixed, standing on the edge of a precipice which represents the dangerous lure of the passions raging within them. When Julie faints she is held by Olivier, only one of two principals for whom the climb may have been uneventful and who remains steady on his feet.

One of Fromentin's best settings is Dominique's impression of Ormesson and his aunt's home. Disturbed by the momentous change taking place in his life and apprehensive about the future, Dominique leaves the rural atmosphere of Trembles for the urban surroundings of Ormesson with considerable trepidation. For one who was accustomed to the freedom and open spaces of nature, the residential, enclosed streets of the town strike him as formidable. As soon as Augustin announces to Mme Ceyssac that he has seen the town, Dominique notes that the countryside is *plat, pâle, fade et mouillé* ("flat, pale, insipid and wet," p. 69). When he hears the sound of the carriage on the pavement and realizes that he is twelve hours from Trembles, he feels that everything is over: ". . . j'entrai dans la maison de Mme Ceyssac comme on franchit le seuil d'une prison."[8] Continuing the image of the prison, Fromentin emphasizes the size of the house (*vaste maison*), uses the word *désert* in reference to the quarter, and stresses the general feeling of constraint in space and values:

C'était une vaste maison, située dans le quartier non pas le plus désert, mais le plus sérieux de la ville, confinant à des couvents, avec un très-petit jardin qui moisissait dans l'ombre de ses hautes clôtures, de grandes chambres sans air et sans vue, des vestibules sonores, un escalier de pierre tournant dans une cage obscure, et trop peu de gens pour animer tout cela. On y sentait la froideur des moeurs anciennes et la rigidité des moeurs de province. . . .[9]

A reflection of his misery is the description of his first day of class in the somber building with the falling rain reminding him of Trembles. But it was not Mme Ceyssac's house alone which he found unappealing. Ormesson itself seemed to him a town more dead than alive:

Imaginez une très-petite ville, dévote, attristée, vieillotte, oubliée dans un fond de province, ne menant nulle part, ne servant à rien, d'où la vie se retirait de jour en jour, et que la campagne envahissait; une industrie nulle, un commerce mort, une bourgeoisie vivant étroitement de ses ressources, une aristocratie qui boudait; le jour, des rues sans mouvement; la nuit, des avenues sans lumières; un silence hargneux, interrompu seulement par des sonneries d'église.[10]

If the emphasis is on the narrowness of life both physical and spiritual, Fromentin even finds an appropriate image in the tree-lined streets: "De longs boulevards, plantés d'ormeaux très-beaux, très-sombres, l'entouraient d'une ombre sévère."[11] Even when Dominique went down to the river, there was no relief from the stifling atmosphere:

On y respirait, dans les vents humides, des odeurs de goudron, de chanvre, et de planches de sapin. Tout cela était monotone et laid. . . .[12]

II *Images and Symbols*

Generally speaking *Dominique* is not a book in which symbols and imagery play a large role. Paris, the provinces, or the sea take on a general symbolic value as they relate to the characters' lives, but scarcely become important as entities in their own right. In addition to such broad symbols Fromentin creates brief images, such as the windmills or the topped tree, which characterize an individual or a moment in the narrative. These images frequently sum up the essence of the person's character or the moment and represent the distillation process which lay at the heart of Fromentin's aesthetic perspective. The symbols are generally not recurrent because their function is basically revelatory and not active as a molder of values or as a catalyst for the action of the text.

Something of the symbolic nature of Paris is seen already in Dominique's impression of Ormesson. The opposition between Dominique's rural domain (its values, social context, and interaction with nature) and Ormesson is that between an urban setting and the country. The move to Paris, however, adds an additional dimension to the urban/rural clash. Paris is not only urban, it is also corrupt. Whereas Ormesson is described as stifling because of the sober religious values and physical constraints, Paris is portrayed as a city which has a different rhythm altogether. Dominique's first impression of Paris is strikingly different from that of Ormesson:

Nous arrivâmes à Paris le soir. Partout ailleurs il eût été tard. Il pleuvait; il faisait froid. Je n'aperçus d'abord que les rues boueuses, des pavés mouillés, luisants sous le feu des boutiques, le rapide et continuel éclair de voitures qui se croisaient en s'éclaboussant, une multitude de lumières étincelant comme des illuminations sans symétrie dans de longues avenues de maisons noires dont la hauteur me parut prodigieuse. Je fus frappé, je m'en souviens, des odeurs de gaz qui annonçaient une ville où l'on vivait la nuit autant que le jour, et de la pâleur des visages qui m'aurait fait croire qu'on s'y portait mal.[13]

Whereas Ormesson would be silent and closed at this hour, Paris is filled with the activity of carriages and flickering lights. Despite the late hour, the rain and the cold, carriages continually rush through the muddy streets. What struck Dominique most and really characterizes the impression, however, is the odor of gas. It symbolizes the unnatural, all-night life of Paris and explains why the inhabitants did not look good. He realizes that he is out of place and it is one of his early warnings that Olivier and he have different roots.

Something has already been said about the lighthouse as a symbol of the dangers of passion and one might include Dominique's room as a kind of tower of danger. The memories locked within this sanctuary remain a threat to Dominique's current peace of mind. They must remain in the past to be revived only when he chooses. Dominique is the kind of person who could easily mistake the past for the present and begin to live exclusively in his memories.

Fromentin uses the flowers which M. de Nièvres sends and the bouquet of flowers at the opera as focal points for the action. When the rhododendrons sent by M. de Nièvres arrive, Madeleine pays little attention to them or the name of the sender. Fromentin stresses that the sender had obviously taken great pains in preparing the bouquet and that M. d'Orsel took special care of them. The flowers are symbolic of the nature of the marriage and relationship between Madeleine and the husband her father selected for her. A second bouquet of flowers plays a symbolic role in the opera scene of chapter 15. After an ecstatic evening near Madeleine, Dominique accompanies her home in the carriage. He notes that she is disturbed and feels certain that the cause of her behavior is her love for him. When she steps down from the carriage, she drops the bouquet. Dominique returns it to her. Madeleine breathes deeply into the bouquet, tells Dominique to cease torturing her, and throws half the bouquet at him. Madeleine is torn by her love for Dominique and is tortured by his efforts to force her to admit her love. The torn bouquet becomes symbolic of their love and the searing effect it is having on Madeleine.

Because of his tendency to see a correspondence between man and his surroundings, it is not surprising that he saw the essential characteristics of Dominique in the tree deliberately cut off at the top to strengthen the development of its root system and increase the amount of shade it could give. The image certainly is appropriate to the life which Dominique has chosen to live.[14] And perhaps the image conveys in less emotional terms the choice between the life he has decided to live and the life he might have chosen in Paris. Many critics are unable to accept the choice he made, because they identify his current life with what they consider bourgeois values and see what he has renounced as a nobler path. By the image of the tree Fromentin places the issue into an amoral context. What is the significance of a tree's height if one must sacrifice the shade it could provide? Since Dominique had assessed his talent and had judged that he was incapable of making a lasting contribution, continuation in this direction would have been as inconsequential as the tree's added height.

During Dominique's visit to Augustin's house on the edge of town, the weather is cold and rainy and Dominique is depressed about his current separation from Madeleine. To Dominique's eyes Augustin and his wife live a life of bare subsistence. In addition to the long hours Augustin spends at his profession, he has many household chores to do. Dominique looks out the window and sees two windmills working steadily in the damp cold:

Je me souviens qu'on voyait des fenêtres deux grands moulins à vent qui dépassaient les murs de clôture, et dont les ailes grises, rayées de baguettes sombres, tournaient sans cesse devant les yeux avec une monotonie de mouvement assoupissante.[15]

It is clear that the windmills represent the ceaseless work of Augustin, constantly turning in a circle, going nowhere, but quietly producing. The image is not felicitous and reflects Dominique's own perspective of Augustin's life as much as the reality.

Other symbols are used to characterize brief moments or carry the emotion of an instant. One evening, a week before the marriage, when everyone is together, M. de Nièvres holds out his two hands to Madeleine. Dominique places great importance in the gesture that follows. If anyone wondered what Madeleine's own feelings were concerning the forthcoming event, she now, at least for Dominique, indicated to everyone that she is giving herself to M. de Nièvres of her own accord:

Madeleine alors jeta un rapide regard autour d'elle, comme pour nous prendre tous à témoin de ce qu'elle allait faire; puis elle se leva, et, sans prononcer une seule parole, mais en accompagnant ce mouvement d'abandon du plus candide et du plus beau des sourires, elle posa ses deux mains dégantées dans les mains du comte.[16]

If Dominique's interpretation is correct, the gesture is significant. But the narrator gives it added significance by emphasizing that her hands are *dégantées*, thus implying a public giving of the self to M. de Nièvres. In this context it is a sensuous image which has special meaning for Dominique. A similar use is made of the cry of the *courlis de mer* during the wedding night. After his apparently awkward conduct following the wedding, Dominique returned to his room and remained awake until dawn, lost in his thoughts. In the middle of the night he is jarred from his meditation by a piercing sound which resembles *un cri d'ami*:

Vers le milieu de la nuit, j'entendis à travers le toit, à travers la distance, à toute portée de son, un cri bref, aigu, qui, même au plus fort de ces convulsions, me fit battre le coeur comme un cri d'ami. J'ouvris la fenêtre et j'écoutai. C'étaient des courlis de mer qui remontaient avec la marée haut et se dirigeaient à plein vol vers la rivière. Le cri se répéta une ou deux fois. . . .[17]

By morning Dominique must face the fact that Madeleine is indeed M. de Nièvres's wife. The piercing cry of the curlew reminds one of the famous scene in Virgil's *Aeneid* when Dido gives herself to Aeneas and of the similar scene in *Madame Bovary*. The sound is, of course, only the cry of the bird. To Dominique, however, its meaning is only too clear.

III *Silence*

One of the more striking narrative features of *Dominique* and the travel accounts is Fromentin's use of silence. Critics have noted that Fromentin used silence to good effect to set off certain sounds which he wished to highlight and that he often communicated by means of a technique which Nathalie Sarraute calls *sous conversation.*

Anyone who has read much about Fromentin gains the impression that his reserve and discretion were manifestations of a shy, private person, one used to being alone with his own thoughts. Although he was reputed to have been an active conversationalist once engaged, he was not the kind of person to speak easily about personal matters. For such an individual the confessional novel could not have been a convenient vehicle for self expression. It is no wonder that Fromentin did not use the conveniences that the omniscient novelist has at his disposal. In fact, he deliberately retained all the doubts and ambiguity of real life, even to the extent that he avoided the clarification which the other characters might have provided. The novel presents a protagonist who describes his awakening to love and subsequent love affair. The difficulty for Dominique as an adolescent is his ignorance of life, a fact which prevents his understanding many statements, gestures, and events which could have clarified the situation for him and made him understand the experiences he was having. Although both Augustin and Olivier provide examples of behavior and give him advice, Dominique is unable to discuss the truly important questions with them, partly because of his natural reticence and embarrassment to discuss such matters and partly because he did not know how to discuss the matter.

As a result, one of the most significant narrative aspects of the text is Fromentin's use of silence. Essentially man is a lonely creature, his thoughts and feelings locked within his own being. Even when he attempts to communicate, his language does not always express exactly what he feels or thinks and, even if it does, it may not be understood correctly by his listener. Furthermore, how can one ever be sure that the other person really understands and how can one really know that he understands what another means? This natural isolation is exacerbated in the novel by the nature of the situation and the values of the people involved: the two lovers must understand one another without an open declaration. Any acknowledgment of love would force a separation, in that they could no longer see one another without admitting the illicit nature of their conduct.

Thus one of the most interesting aspects of the novel is Fromentin's use of silence as a context for or barrier to understanding. This involves the reader as well as the character in the novel, because there is no certain source of knowledge. Although Dominique understands some of the circumstances better than he did twenty years ago, he still remains doubtful about much that concerns himself and the others. In the initial chapter, when the name of Paris comes up, Dominique exclaims, "Encore des regrets!" The narrator comments that he said it with a special emphasis that made him wish to know what he meant by it. The reader too is perplexed. To what extent does Paris represent regret for Dominique and how actively does the regret affect his current happiness? The remainder of the novel never really clears up the issue. It is doubtful whether Dominique himself could answer the question.[18]

In a number of instances Dominique comes to understand himself or events in moments of silence or through an interpretation of a look or gesture. Dominique's awakening to the fact that he has fallen in love is a good example. He is unaware of the cause of his restlessness in chapter 5; in fact he does not even suspect that there might be a cause until his aunt takes him under the light to look at him closely. His uneasiness at her scrutiny represents a first awareness. Later he meets Olivier with Julie and Madeleine. The meeting takes him by such surprise that he departs abruptly. Olivier questions him about his reaction and Dominique gives the weak excuse that he was not feeling well and that Olivier should beg Madeleine's pardon for him. Olivier's reply that one need not answer to Madeleine and his knowing smile cause Dominique to realize that he is under scrutiny, that Olivier is seeking a cause for his recent behavior. For the first time Dominique begins to look within himself for the reason. At dinner Dominique does not sit in his regular place next to Madeleine, pretending to himself that the light there bothers him. Madeleine immediately notices that he is in an unaccustomed place across from her. She is about to make comment when their eyes meet. The exchange of looks is revealing to both. How much Madeleine understands is uncertain, since later in the text she seems not fully aware of Dominique's feelings toward her, but she recognizes that any comment on her part would embarrass the sensitive Dominique. On his part he knows immediately what his problem is and he now understands why people remark on the beauty of Madeleine, something he had earlier repeated without conviction. Now Dominique is certain. Looking in her eyes is "comme une révélation définitive qui compléta les révélations des jours précédents, les réunit pour ainsi dire en un faisceau d'évidences, et, je crois, les expliqua toutes."[19]

One of the most memorable examples of Fromentin's ability to present a tableau in words provides the setting from which Dominique learns of Madeleine's future marriage. After Madeleine's return and the arrival of the flowers from M. de Nièvres, several months pass and winter approaches. With the approach of the cold weather,[20] Dominique notices a change in Madeleine: ". . . je crus apercevoir sur le visage de Madeleine une ombre et comme un souci qui n'y avait jamais paru."[21] She is as cordial and affectionate as ever, but by her silence, sudden departures, and general reticence Dominique feels that something has come between them for the first time. He remembers the name of the stranger and has a momentary apprehension. Three days pass without seeing any of his friends. Dominique goes to their home and finds them all in the salon seriously engaged in a family discussion and formally dressed. One person in the room is a stranger to Dominique. Fromentin describes the scene so vividly and analyzes its composition so well that one feels as if one were standing before a painting. Dominique looks down on the scene from a high window outside the room. M. d'Orsel and a stranger of thirty-five sit opposite one another. Olivier, dressed in black, stood by the fireplace. Madeleine is seated at a table working on her crewel, while Julie sits, her hands in her lap and her eyes fixed on the stranger. Perhaps the view of Madeleine is what illuminates the scene:

Je la vois encore, la tête un peu penchée sur sa tapisserie, le visage envahi par l'ombre de ses cheveux bruns, enveloppée dans le reflet rougissant des lampes.[22]

Although Madeleine's face and expression are not visible to us because of the shadow from her hair, the reflection of the lamps tells Dominique everything he dreaded to know:

Ce que je vous dis là, je m'en rendis compte en quelques secondes. Puis il me semble que les lumières s'éteignaient.[23]

During the interlude at Trembles when Dominique and Madeleine spend two carefree months together there is no disclosure between the two concerning their love. The reader and Dominique are uncertain what Madeleine knows or suspects. There is no reserve in her attitude toward him, yet one wonders how the earlier indications which she perceived did not awaken her to Dominique's love. However, when she mentions that the time has come for them to return to Paris and Dominique expresses a *dèjà* that is full of regret, Madeleine seems to become suspicious of the truth, as if it were the first indication she had. She watches him closely for awhile and he does all to allay her suspicions. Then, when they are about to leave and Dominique expresses regret at losing what he has had at Trembles, she answers: "Mon ami, vous êtes un ingrat!"[24] Just what she means by that and how much she understands is never made clear.

There are several instances in the text where Dominique describes actions and gestures which may be very significant but whose meaning is left unclear because one is not certain that Dominique has interpreted them correctly. During the wild ride through the forest, provoked by Madeleine, who insisted that Dominique ride her husband's horse, Madeleine deliberately leads Dominique on a dangerous chase which evokes the potential illicit love affair which they are nearly caught up in. At one point Dominique catches up to her and finds her waiting at a crossroad:

Arrivé juste à l'endroit où elle avait disparu, je la trouvai dans l'entrecroisement de deux routes, arrêtée, haletante, et m'attendant le sourire aux lèvres.[25]

When one considers Madeleine's smile, that she is waiting for him at the crossroads, and that she is described as *haletante*, one wonders what she intends. Dominique scolds her and tells her to stop or he would kill himself. Madeleine's response is significant:

Elle me répondit seulement par un regard direct qui m'empourpra le visage, et reprit plus posément l'allée du château. Nous revînmes au pas, sans échanger une seule parole. . . ."[26]

What is the meaning of Madeleine's look into Dominique's eyes? She immediately calms down and takes the path which leads back to the chateau. Is there a deliberate suggestion here that the other path led away from the chateau and represented the path of their illicit love? Was Madeleine waiting to take that path, if only she were urged by Dominique? Then one might ask what Dominique understood by her actions. His own statement seems designed to make her stop her wild ride. It seems likely that he had in mind only her danger. These questions really remain unanswered and other actions by Madeleine in the chapter only add to one's doubt. When they return from the ride, she goes straight to her room and remains. One wonders what her thoughts are. Why does she go to her room when M. de Nièvres's letter arrives announcing that he will not return for a month? And what does she mean when she asks Dominique to help her join the ends of her shawl? Dominique would have Madeleine struggling against her own love and he believes that, if Madeleine were to yield, she would die of remorse. The shroud of silence which envelops many important moments in the action allows the motivation of Dominique and Madeleine to remain obscure.

Some find Dominique's reason for not taking Madeleine poorly motivated. Fromentin has been developing the motif of bestiality in the text, that Dominique's reason was being dominated by his senses. Fromentin is careful to say that the pity which caused him to refrain from taking Madeleine had nothing to do with a final victory of reason over the senses. The pity he felt did not stem from a rational, conscious process. Rather, within the beast there was yet a basic instinct which caused him to withdraw from the prey as soon as it had surrendered itself in anticipation of the final death-blow. Right or wrong, Dominique's belief that Madeleine would die should she yield lends a certain logic to the development of the text as he constructed it.

Finally, silence is used by Madeleine as a defense in her attempt to retain Dominique's friendship without entering into an illicit affair. Much of the novel after the marriage develops the attempt of Dominique to force Madeleine to acknowledge her love. Armand Hoog[27] argues that Fromentin's novel is *un livre cruel* masked by a romanesque veneer:

Pour qui fait un peu attention, *Dominique* devient le roman même de la plaie et du couteau.[28]

Without agreeing with the psychological implications which Hoog sees in terms of Fromentin's own life, one can agree in part with his assessment of one aspect of the book. In his desire for Madeleine, Dominique cruelly tortures her on several occasions only to withdraw when he reduces her to tears and a kind of defenseless state. He is filled with remorse on each occasion, but his instinctive desire for her causes him to return after a short respite.[29] The image of self-torture implied by Hoog in his comparison of the book to Baudelaire's *Héautontimoroumenos* is reflected in much of Dominique's behavior. He strives to force Madeleine to acknowledge her love, yet he knows the consequences can only cause him pain: either this will end their companionship or Madeleine will enter into complicity and suffer remorse. Throughout the text Madeleine tries to preserve their love by pretending that it is not a question of love. It is as if she would continue their love in a state of suspension neither acknowledging that they love one another nor conducting themselves as lovers. Caught in this precarious situation, Madeleine uses various forms of silence cleverly to preserve the illusion that she does not know that Dominique loves her. When Dominique is melancholy and speaks of his depression, Madeleine realizes that she must not inquire as to the cause of his melancholy, lest she give him the opportunity to declare himself. When Dominique is more pointed in his references, Madeleine evidently pretends not to understand his innuendo or double meaning and answers him literally and naively.

After a few weeks' absence Dominique returns to Madeleine unannounced. He finds her sewing. Her eyes are red, as if she had been crying. When he sees how pitiful she is, his resolve to conquer her weakens and he apologizes to her. Madeleine, of course, cannot pretend to understand the need for an apology, so she tells him not to apologize when none is needed. However, she reproaches him for remaining absent thirty days, thus letting him know that she has counted the days. To deflect the conversation from a dangerous subject, she asks him to recount his activities. Dominique refuses to elaborate and returns to a line of conversation which will lead to a declaration. Finally, when Madeleine's verbal resources have been exhausted, she sits in silence, tears streaming down her cheeks, and then leaves. Madeleine's defense is silence and her ultimate defense resembles that used by the Princesse de Clèves. After informing Dominique that they must separate permanently, she acknowledges her love for him, thus thwarting any future possibility of a visit. Once she admits her love, she cannot see him innocently, as if he were merely an old friend.

CHAPTER 11

Conclusion

BECAUSE Fromentin was part of the second generation of Romantics, he is a particularly enlightening figure to study as an index to the period. Raised on the literature of the Romantic period, he shared the typical hero's love of solitude, identification with nature, and private, poetic world of the senses. But the nineteenth century, for all its reaction against Classicism, had not yet abandoned the basic premises of the Classical aesthetic. The sense of the absolute and emphasis on form still played an important role in French aesthetic thought. The Romantic sensibility had ushered in superficial variations which, initially, did not destroy the concept of an absolute reality which transcended this world. Eventually Realism, with its materialistic orientation, would reject the basic premise of the Classical tradition.

Fromentin reached manhood at the crossroads of this tradition. By the 1840s French Neoclassicism was experiencing a revival after the heady years of Romantic fervor. But the trend of painting toward objective naturalism and the growing dominance of the Realistic/ Naturalistic novel insured the brevity of the revival. As a Romantic sensibility with a Classical formation, Fromentin perceived that art must strike a balance between the Romantic and Classic modes. His Classical training taught him to respect the masters and to place a premium on style, something they alone could teach. Yet he also shared the modern insistence on the mimetic role of art and the importance of nature to art. In the modern attitude, however, Fromentin saw the germs of destruction. The interest in nature threatened to undermine art. For Fromentin the slavish imitation of reality subordinated art to the copy, set subject matter over form, and elevated truth over beauty. In his novel, painting, travel literature, and criticism he attempted to find the absolute. Fromentin looked for the underlying permanence in a changing world. He sought the harmony and order of autumn, which, in its harvest, benefits from the turmoil of spring and yet avoids the stagnation of winter.

140

Notes and References

Chapter One

1. The autobiographical details of *Dominique* will be discussed in chapter 6.
2. About fifty pages remain from this incomplete study.
3. Marilhat's exposition of 1844 played a decisive role in awakening Fromentin's interest in a new treatment of Oriental subjects.
4. Bataillard was unable to bring himself to be a party to the ruse and never sent the letters.
5. The occasion for the trip was the marriage of Charles Labbé's sister at Blida.
6. According to stories neither Fromentin's mother nor his father ever really approved his artistic career. Despite his success, both parents always lamented that he had not followed a career in law.
7. The du Mesnils were of noble extraction and lost their fortune during the Revolution. Marie's father was from a family of old nobility. He retired from the army to his family estate. Whereas his son lived with him, he confided his daughter to the care of Mme du Mesnil, her grandmother.
8. The collection of thirty letters and nearly as many replies covers the years 1857 to 1866, with several important lacunae (principally July 1859–April 1862 and July 1863–August 1865). From 1866 to 1876, when both writers died, no correspondence remains.
9. Isidore-Augustin Pils (1813–1875) was elected in his place.
10. "The mechanical tracing of an object, photography for example, will it give us a better idea of the reality of the object? What will it teach us about the very essence of the real? Nothing more, since commenting on the absolute nature of things is difficult when dealing with the image as the object itself" (Pierre Blanchon, *Correspondance et fragments inédits* [Paris, 1912], pp. 389–90. Hereafter cited as Blanchon, *Correspondance*).
11. Fromentin made a belated effort to gain the vacant seat on the Académie Française. He lost to the art critic Charles Blanc (1813–1882), but obtained twelve votes despite his late start.

Chapter Two

1. Marie-Anne Eckstein, *Le Rôle du souvenir dans l'oeuvre d'Eugène Fromentin* (Zurich, 1970).

2. ". . . To tame the passion by transforming the loved one into another being like himself" (Eckstein, p. 64).

3. ". . . Fromentin deliberately destroys the exterior of a man who has lived only too much on the surface of himself . . ." (ibid., p. 70).

4. ". . . I wish to penetrate deeply into the intimacy of this people. . . . It is the small detail of domestic life, of the uses, of the customs that I wish to learn. I wish all that to become as familiar to me as our European life" (Pierre Blanchon, *Lettres de Jeunesse* [Paris, 1908], p. 240).

5. ". . . It is the poetic and intimate side of things which strikes me and which I wish to grasp" (ibid.).

6. "What is the *subject* if not the anecdote introduced into art, the fact instead of the plastic idea, the narrative when there is a narrative, the scene, the exactness of costume, the verisimilitude of the effect, in a word, the truth, whether historic or picturesque? Everything follows, everything is connected. Logic brought to the *subject* leads straight to local color, that is to say, to an impasse, for art can go no further. It is finished" (Eugène Fromentin, *Une Année dans le Sahel* [Paris, 1877], pp. 206–207).

7. "The painter who will boldly decide to be realistic at all costs will bring back something so new from his travels, so difficult to determine that, the *artistic* dictionary not having any appropriate term for works of such an unexpected character, I shall call this category of subjects *documents*" (ibid., p. 215).

8. "The exterior world is like a dictionary. It is a book filled with repetitions and synonyms: many equivalent words for the same idea. The ideas are simple, the forms multiple. It is for us to choose and summarize" (ibid., p. 7).

9. "It was very beautiful and in this unexpected union of costume and statuary, of pure form and barbaric fantasy, there was an example of detestable but dazzling taste to follow. Besides, let's not speak of taste concerning such a subject. For today let's forget the rules. It is a question of a tableau without order and which has almost nothing in common with art. Let's refrain from discussing it; let's just watch" (ibid., p. 184).

10. As Fromentin commented in a slightly different context: "Il est exceptionnel, et l'histoire atteste que rien de beau ni de durable n'a été fait avec des exceptions" (It is exceptional and history attests that nothing beautiful nor durable has been made with exceptions [ibid., p. 214]).

11. Another example is the judgment on the mixed architectural face of Algiers. The contrast between the older Arab structures and the newly constructed French buildings lacks harmony and proportion. The beauty of either form can be brought out only when the clash between styles is eliminated.

12. In discussing how ungainly the boys look, Fromentin mentions a detail which he would ordinarily not include in his description of the mores: ". . . me permettras-tu ce détail, un peu trop local? des paquets de mouches fixés aux coins des yeux, des narines et des lèvres . . ." (. . . will you allow me a detail which is a little too local? clusters of flies attached to the corners of the

eyes, the nostrils and the lips . . . [Eugène Fromentin, *Un Eté dans le Sahara* (Paris, 1877), p. 145].

13. ". . . An art which consisted in making a choice from things, in embellishing them, in altering them; an art which lived in the absolute rather than in the relative, perceived nature as it is but took pleasure in portraying it otherwise. Everything more or less pertained to mankind, depended upon him, was subordinate to him and was modeled on him. . . . There resulted a kind of universal humanity or a humanized universe of which the human body, in its ideal proportions, was the prototype" (Eugène Fromentin, *Maîtres d'autrefois*. Edited with introduction and notes by Pierre Moisy [Paris, 1972], p. 115).

14. "Nature existed vaguely around this absorbing personage" (ibid.).

15. "An admirable and overwhelming thing, nature details and summarizes everything at the same time. We are only capable of summarizing at most, happy when we know how to do it. Small minds prefer detail. Only the masters are on good terms with nature. They have observed it so much that in their turn they make it understood. They have learned from nature the secret of simplicity, which is the key to so many mysteries" (*Un Eté*, p. 70).

16. "Is it children playing in the sun? Is it a place in the sun where children are playing? The question is not irrelevant, for it points out two very different points of view. In the first case, it is a painting of figures where the landscape is considered an accessory. In the second it is a landscape where the human figure is subordinate, set in the background, in a sacrificial role" (*Une Année*, p. 211).

17. In addition to Eckstein, see Margaret Mein, *A Foretaste of Proust. A Study of Proust and his Precursors* (Farnborough, Hants, 1974), pp. 143–60, and Jacques Monge, "Un Précurseur de Proust: Fromentin et la mémoire affective." *Revue d'Histoire Littéraire de la France* (1961), p. 564–88. For Fromentin's use of memory see Waltrud Kappeler, *Fromentin, ein Dichter der Erinnerung* (Wintherthur-Töss, 1949).

18. "Dominique's mania for dates and categories comes to him, therefore, from his preoccupation with retaining the moments of consciousness and the care not to lose sight of oneself" (Eckstein, p. 14).

19. "To remember thus is to become accustomed to an awareness by which one grasps his inner unity. It is not the past which resurges through time that separates it from us, but the being which one was in the past and which comes to melt into the sameness of the being that one is" (ibid., p. 17).

20. "It rendered me all kinds of services. It especially forced me to seek the truth outside of exactness and resemblance outside of the precise copy" (*Un Eté*, p. x).

21. "It is an irresistible pleasure to say about a country which few people have visited: I have seen it. . . . One must be more modest yet—and this modesty becomes a principle of art—to summarize so many precious notes into one painting, to sacrifice the satisfaction of one's own memories to the vague search for a general and uncertain goal. Let's speak literally, a true

renunciation of oneself is necessary to hide one's studies and to show of them only the result" (*Une Année*, pp. 216–17).

22. "Memories are of a marvelous lucidity. They are connected and developed, they multiply or sum up with perfect order. The dark areas of life are clarified, the myseries of the heart are uncovered, so much is our inner being illuminated. . . . Finally, the indefinite perspectives of time opening all at once . . . the unknown itself is revealed and allows itself to be perceived. Judgments on the past are exact, forecasts are nearly infallible" (Blanchon, *Lettres*, p. 126).

23. "In passing through the memory, the truth becomes a poem, the landscape a painting. However large or beautiful reality may be, you will see that memory ends by surpassing it and succeeds in embellishing it. I am certain that everything I saw three months ago is now inferior to the transformed image which I have kept of it . . ." (ibid., p. 191).

Chapter Three

1. "It had seemed that the future of painting would be tied to the predominance of line over color or of beauty over character. These questions, without being resolved, were going to become of secondary importance. It is another problem, equally eternal, that of the legitimate relationship between art and society, which was going to stimulate enthusiasm and anger" (Léon Rosenthal, *Du Romantisme au Réalisme* [Paris: Renouard, 1914], p. 348). Rosenthal's volume is still a good introduction to Romanticism despite a marked assumption that post-eighteenth-century aesthetic values are superior to what preceded. A splendid study of the trend toward Realism in French art, especially as it is focused around Courbet and Manet, is Joseph Sloane's *French Painting Between the Past and Present* (Princeton, N.J., 1951). The value of Linda Nochlin's *Realism and Tradition in Art 1848–1900* (Englewood Cliffs, N.J.: Prentice-Hall, 1966) is considerably diminished by the presentation of material through the perspective of her own aesthetic bias. Elizabeth Holt provides a convenient collection of source materials in *From the Classicists to the Impressionists: Art and Architecture in the Nineteenth Century* (Garden City: Doubleday, 1966).

2. Among other factors, the economic situation precluded the continued prominence of the large canvas. The bourgeois clientele neither had space for such paintings nor the educational background to appreciate the heavily literary, symbolic context. Portrait painting increased with a growing demand from the bourgeois clientele and the greater attention given to realism in art tended to encourage contemporary subjects of humbler origin.

3. J. B. Deperthès, *Théorie du paysage* (Paris, 1818).

4. Charles Bigot, *Peintres français contemporains* (Paris: Hachette, 1888), p. 86.

5. Letter to Lilia Beltrémieux on September 17, 1849. Cited in Blanchon, *Correspondance*, pp. 7–9.

6. "These are studies on nature, rapid and, by consequence, of broad treatment, summary and even coarse, of clear character and incisive, with the dominant trait set in relief. The extremities, the hands and feet, are barely indicated, but the movement is right, cursory, in many cases exquisitely eloquent" (Gonse, p. 54).

7. Henry Houssaye, "Eugène Fromentin: l'exposition de son oeuvre à l'Ecole des Beaux-Arts," *Revue des Deux Mondes* (1877), p. 885.

8. *Un Eté*, pp. 55–56. See note twenty of chapter 4 for further discussion of this contrast.

9. ". . . The two most intelligent and most perfect creatures (in terms of form) that God has made" (*Une Année*, p. 268).

10. ". . . Mingle man with the horse, give to the torso initiative and will, give to the rest of the body the combined attributes of quickness and vigor, and you have a supremely strong being, thinking and acting, courageous and quick, free and submissive" (ibid., p. 268).

11. Maxime Du Camp, *Souvenirs littéraires*, Vol. 2 (Paris, 1892), pp. 200–206.

12. ". . . Would have preferred to be a history painter . . ."; ". . . he always dreamed of going from real life and anecdotes to the ideal and the epic" (Gonse, p. 82).

13. "This spectacle awaits its painter. Only one man today would know how to understand it and translate it. He alone would have the imaginative ingenuity and power, the boldness and the right to try it" (*Une Année*, p. 268).

14. "Finally, something not less serious, I see *joli* and not *grand*; of all my failings that is perhaps the one which distresses me most because it is an inner defect which will never be totally correctible" (letter of November 12, 1847, Blanchon, *Lettres*, p. 250–51).

15. Maxime Du Camp, p. 202.

Chapter Four

1. In a June 1846 letter to his mother he writes: "Je n'ai pas le don d'inventer ce que je n'ai pas vu, et il faut être sobre d'hypothèses en fait d'art dans la reproduction du vrai et même du possible" (Blanchon, *Lettres*, p. 182). "I do not have the gift of inventing what I have not seen and one must be careful about guessing when it is a question of reproducing the true or even the possible in art." The following year, on 13 August 1847, he wrote to his father in an effort to explain that he was not minimizing study and imitation of the masters, but that experience with the reality one is painting is also extremely important (ibid., pp. 223–27).

2. Letter to Armand du Mesnil from Blida, 29 August 1853. Blanchon, *Correspondance,* pp. 78–80.

3. ". . . The insufficiency of my craft advised me, as an expedient, to seek another. The difficulty of painting with the brush made me try the pen" (*Un Eté,* p. v).

4. "There is no question but what the plastic art has its laws, its limits, its conditions necessary for existence, what one calls, briefly, its domain" (ibid., p. viii).

5. "There are forms which suit the mind as there are forms which are suitable for the eyes; the language which speaks to the eyes is not the same as that which speaks to the mind. And the book is there to repeat the work of the painter, but to express what it (the painting) does not say" (ibid., pp. viii–ix).

6. The fragment appeared in the July, August, and September issues.

7. Blanchon, *Correspondance,* p. 79.

8. Haoûa cannot be identified with any particular person Fromentin knew or met during his travels. Fouad Marcos points out that the word Haoûa can have several meanings depending upon where one places the accent and how one pronounces the word. He suggests that Haoûa was intended as a composite idealization of the Arab woman. Louis Vandell is the fictional name for Oscar MacCarthy (Fouad Marcos, *Fromentin et l'Afrique* [Montreal, 1973]).

9. "Les Descriptions de Fromentin," *Revue Africaine* (1910), pp. 343–92.

10. In his long discussion of art, motivated by Vandell's realistic drawings, Fromentin places the blame for the decline of art on "la curiosité et le goût des anecdotes" (the curiosity and taste for anecdotes [p. 205]). See the discussion of chapter 2.

11. Obviously these commentaries would serve him well when he sought to paint his African scenes from memory. They preserved the meaning, tone, and atmosphere which made the scene or moment memorable and significant.

12. "This shadow in the countries of light, you know it. It is inexpressible, dark and transparent, clear and yet tinted, like deep water. It appears black, but when the eye penetrates it, one is surprised to see clearly. Delete the sun and the shadow itself will become daylight. Figures float there in a kind of light atmosphere which makes contours disappear" (*Un Eté,* p. 149).

13. "El-Kantara—the bridge—watches over the pass and only gateway to the Sahara from the Tell. This passageway is a narrow cleft that one would say is man-made in an enormous wall of stone some three to four hundred feet high. The bridge, which is of Roman construction, spans the gorge. Having crossed the bridge and taken one hundred steps into the pass, suddenly you come upon a charming village down a steep slope. It is watered by a deep river and is lost in a forest of twenty-five thousand palms. You are in the Sahara" (ibid., p. 4).

14. "It is also an established belief among the Arabs that the mountain stops all the clouds of the Tell at its summit, that the rain is stopped by it and the winter never crosses the miraculous bridge, which thus divides two seasons, winter and summer, and two regions, the Tell and the Sahara. They offer as proof that one side of the mountain is black and the color of rain, while the other is pink and the color of fair weather" (ibid., p. 5).

15. "This unexpected crossing from one season to the other, the strangeness of the place, the newness of the perspective—everything united to make of it a kind of raising of a splendid curtain. This sudden appearance of the Orient through the golden door of El-Kantara always left me with a memory which seemed linked to the supernatural" (ibid., p. 9).

16. "It appears very small and hugs the two flanks of the town with the appearance of wishing to defend it in time of need . . ." (ibid., p. 180).

17. ". . . It resembles two gardens of leaves surrounded by a long wall, like a park, and sketched roughly against the barren plain" (ibid.). Fromentin finds an additional symbol of the nature of this country in the sharp contrast afforded by the old man and young girl whom he encounters during the trip.

18. "The composition [of the dinner] is consecrated by usage and has become a formality. To dispense with the details once and for all, here is the basic menu of a *diffa* prepared according to the traditional format" (ibid., p. 18).

19. ". . . You must understand that the act of eating and serving is a serious thing among the Arabs and that a *diffa* is a supreme lesson in living, in generosity, and in mutual kindnesses. And notice that it is not because of social duty, an absolutely unknown concept to this antisocial people, but because of divine injunction and, to speak their language, as emissaries of God that the traveler is so treated by his host. Therefore, their politeness is not based on convention, but on a religious principle. They exercise it with the respect which they have for all that touches holy things and they practice it as an act of piety" (ibid., p. 20).

20. Another contrast Fromentin sees in the Arab is his lethargy and laziness on the one hand and, on the other, his avidity for combat and energetic activity when it comes to fighting on horseback. In fact, the contrast between the Arab on foot and the Arab on horseback is what, in Fromentin's eyes, distinguishes the biblical figure from the epic warrior:

. . . Rien ne se ressemble moins que ces deux hommes, suivant qu'ils sont à pied ou à cheval. En quoi ils diffèrent n'est pas aisé à définir, mais peut-être me comprendras-tu quand je te dirai que l'un est plus historique que l'autre. L'Arabe à pied, drapé, chaussé de sandales, est l'homme de tous les temps et de tous les pays; de la Bible, si tu veux. . . Le cavalier, au contraire, debout sur son cheval efflanqué, lui serrant les côtes, lui rendant la bride, poussant un cri du gosier et partant au galop, penché sur le cou de sa bête, une main à l'arçon de la selle, l'autre au fusil, voilà l'homme du Sahara; tout au plus, pourrait-on le confondre avec le cavalier de Syrie.

. . . Nothing is less alike than these two men depending on whether they are on foot or on horseback. It is not easy to define how they differ, but perhaps you will understand me when I say that the one is more historical than the other. The Arab on foot, clothed, wearing sandals, is the man of all time and all countries, the man of the Bible, if you wish. . . . The horseman, contrarily, seated on his lean horse squeezing his sides, giving him his head, crying out and galloping away, bent over on the neck of his steed, one hand on the saddle horn the other on his gun—that is the man of the Sahara. One could confuse him with the horseman of Syria. (*Un Eté*, p. 155)

21. "To see these robust men in their garments of war and with charms around their necks fulfilling seriously minor household tasks which are a woman's work in Europe is not a sight which provokes laughter. To see these large hands hardened by handling horses and the use of weapons serve at table, slice the meat before offering it to you, indicate the portions of the mutton which are cooked best, hold the ewer or present the towel of worked wool is not a laughing matter. These attentions, which would appear puerile or ridiculous according to our customs, become touching here by the contrast which exists between the man and the petty uses which he makes of his strength and dignity" (ibid., pp. 20–21).

22. "But to that they answered that, if the Beni l'Aghouat have seen the new moon, it is because they looked at it less closely than elsewhere. In Aïn-Mahdy they were more precise; the fast was still in effect." (ibid., p. 252).

23. Fromentin describes Laghouat, Tadjemout, and Aïn-Mahdy as dead places. The recent conquest by the French has left the fortified town prostrate. In their isolation and desolation they resemble the desert itself, half dead in the silence and heat of mid-afternoon.

24. "The silence is one of the subtlest charms of this solitary, empty country. It communicates to the soul a stability which you who have always lived in tumult cannot know" (ibid., p. 66).

25. "If I can compare the sensations of hearing to those of sight, the silence spread over the great spaces is a kind of airy transparence which heightens perception and opens to us an unknown world of infinitely small sounds; it reveals an expanse of inexpressible pleasures. I am filled thus, all my senses satisfied, with the happiness of living as a nomad" (ibid., pp. 66–67).

26. ". . . by a continuous echo reaching to the end of the plains" (*Une Année*, p. 76).

27. ". . . The immobility of this solid sea then becomes more striking than ever. In seeing it begin at one's feet then stretch out and plunge to the south, the east, and the west without trace of road or any modulation [in the terrain], one wonders about the nature of this silent country, clothed in an uncertain tone which seems the color of the void. from which no one comes and where no one goes and which ends by a clear, straight line against the sky" (*Un Eté*, p. 182).

28. "I have before me the beginning of this enigma and the spectacle is strange under this clear noonday sun. It is here that I would like to see the Egyptian Sphinx" (ibid., p. 183).

29. The only comparable thing in *Un Eté* was Fromentin's inclusion of his experience with Ahmet, the Arab servant who stole his money. This is the only attempt to create a personal relationship. The military officer with whom he spends much of his time is not developed as a personality and is only mentioned in passing.

30. In his attempt to give unity to *Une Année* Fromentin added thematic touches which relate to the story of Haoûa and her impending death. On three occasions he is preoccupied with death, once in mentioning the cemetery of Sid-Abd-el-Kader, a second in reference to the cemeteries of the dead who paid dearly for France to acquire the grain production once owned by Rome, and a third when he walks through the cemetery and reflects on death prior to his regular visits to Haoûa. Fromentin introduces the hashish smoker Naman, whose death and burial occur near the beginning of book three. In another instance Fromentin describes the execution by firing squad and once meditates on the relationship between the winter and the coming rain. Even the sowing of the fields prior to the winter rains causes one to recognize the life cycle and the fact that, if life ends in death, it also stems from it.

31. "The only interest which, in my eyes, they have not lost and which attaches them to my present life is a certain way of seeing, feeling, and expressing myself which is personal and continues to be mine. They say nearly what I was and I continue to see myself in them. I also find there what I dreamed of being, with promises which have not all been kept and intentions which, for the most part, have not been realized" (*Un Eté*, p. iii).

32. See Martino, "Descriptions".

33. ". . . Besides the word is brutal; it distorts a tone of fineness and which is only an appearance. To express the action of the sun on this burning earth by saying that the ground is yellow is to disfigure and spoil everything" (*Un Eté*, p. 28).

34. ". . . The light, of an incredible brilliance but diffuse, causes neither amazement nor fatigue. It bathes you also with impalpable waves, like a second atmosphere. It envelops without blinding. Besides the brilliance of the sky is softened by such delicate blues. The color of these vast plateaux, covered with a little hay already withered, is so soft, the shadows themselves from all that makes a shadow are drowned in so many reflections that one's sight does not experience any pain. To understand to what extent this light is intense it is almost necessary [to sense it by] reflection" (ibid., p. 67).

35. "I note in passing a painter's remark: contrary to what one sees in Europe, paintings here are composed in shadow with a dark center and light in the corners. It is, to a certain extent, Rembrandt transposed. Nothing is more mysterious" (ibid., p. 149).

36. "To describe an apartment of women or portray Arab religious ceremonies is, in my opinion, more serious than fraud: it is to commit an error in judgment with regard to art" (ibid., p. 261).

37. See the letter from Blida, 8 February, in Part II of *Une Année*.

Chapter Five

1. In 1864 Fromentin was asked to give a public lecture on the aesthetic of modern art. The lecture never took place but portions of a text remain in the writer's extant papers. Louis Gonse, who published the fragments in his *Eugène Fromentin* (Paris, 1881), suggests that the project grew in Fromentin's mind into a larger essay which would include a discussion of Romanticism and the modern school, before providing his own program. Gonse surmises that he turned aside from the study because he feared that it would take him away from projects in which he was already involved.

2. Eugène Fromentin, *Maîtres d'autrefois*, edited by Pierre Moisy (Paris, 1972).

3. "It would be like a kind of conversation on painting in which the painters would recognize their practices and people would learn to evaluate painters and painting better" (*Maîtres*, p. 4).

4. For a general discussion of the influence of the Dutch masters on French painting, see Petra Ten Doesschate Chu, *French Realism and the Dutch Masters* (Utrecht: Dekker & Gumbert, 1974).

5. "I entitle these pages, *Maîtres d'autrefois*, as if to say severe or familiar *masters* of our French language . . ." (*Maîtres*, p. 4).

6. Meyer Schapiro, "Fromentin as a Critic," *Partisan Review* January 1949, p. 29.

7. ". . . A description framed by a general evaluation and a conclusive evaluation." A. Romus, "Fromentin critique d'art," *Marche Romane* 12(1962): 20.

8. Pierre Moreau, *"De la Philosophie de l'art aux Maîtres d'autrefois, ou l'école des sensations,"* in *De Jean Lemaire de Belges à Jean Giraudoux: Mélanges d'histoire et de critique littéraire offerts à Pierre Jourda* (Paris: Nizet, 1970), pp. 359–74. See also the remarks of Pierre Moisy in the introduction to his edition of *Maîtres d'autrefois*.

9. "The moral basis of Dutch art is the total absence of what we call today a *subject*" (*Maîtres*, p. 127).

10. Meyer Schapiro feels that Fromentin's use of antithesis is a basic strength in the work. In Schapiro's contemporary perspective conflict is a basic ingredient in the development of personality, so the dialectical approach is appropriate and makes the work modern.

11. Fromentin enjoys using a rhetorical question based on a previous line of thought only to have the answer he proposes contradict the anticipated

answer. Chapter 6 praises Ruben's ability to paint individual portraits in a group painting. But the question in chapter 7 (Is he a good painter of portraits?) will be answered in the negative. He often enjoys building sentences or paragraphs on opposites which can be developed by contrast. In speaking of Van Veen and Van Noort: "Dans tous les cas, il en est un dont l'action s'explique et ne se voit guère; il en est un autre dont l'action se manifeste sans qu'on l'explique . . ." (In any case there is one whose action can be explained but is scarcely seen and there is another whose action is manifest without being able to explain it . . . [*Maîtres*, p. 22]. One could multiply examples of Fromentin's use of antithesis in syntax and paragraph structure at length.

12. Modern criticism no longer accepts the description and analysis which Fromentin presents of Rubens's teachers.

13. In the development of the myth of creativity, post-eighteenth-century man has tended to place the intellect in opposition to the subconscious, the former being seen as a hindrance to the development of the latter. Fromentin obviously accepts the new myth, but in good classic form he seeks a harmony of the two forces. He does not see the creative impulse in hopeless conflict with learning and training as the post-eighteenth-century aesthetic perspective does.

14. Today often attributed to Van Dyck.

15. Some feel that Fromentin was only trying to offer palliatives which he did not really believe.

16. ". . . This great portrait painter is above all a visionary, this very exceptional colorist is first and foremost a painter of light, his strange atmosphere is the air which is suitable to his ideas and there are, outside of nature or rather in the depths of nature, things which this fisher of pearls alone has discovered" (*Maîtres*, p. 248).

17. "If you diminish my master Rembrandt a little, I pardon you, because, fundamentally, you speak of him lovingly; you speak of him in the manner of a lover who beats his beloved" (Blanchon, *Correspondance*, p. 402, n. 1).

18. The reader is referred to the excellent edition of Professor Moisy. The notes and introduction are most helpful as a corrective to the text.

Chapter Six

1. For a discussion of pastoral elements in *Dominique* and its place in the pastoral tradition, see the articles of Robin Magowan, "Fromentin and Jewett: Pastoral Narrative in the Nineteenth Century," *Comparative Literature* 16(1964): 331–37, and "*Dominique*: The Genesis of a Pastoral," *Esprit Créateur* 13(1973): 340–50.

2. Georges Pailhès, "Le Modèle de *Dominique*," *Revue Bleue* 47(1909): 330, 358–62. Pailhès clearly resented that *Dominique* continued to be read

when, in his view, *Edouard* was a more penetrating novel. He felt that *Dominique* had the fame which *Edouard* should have had.

3. Pailhès makes several comparisons: both heroes go to the lady's room at night, both have a scene involving flowers; in each text an important scene is centered around a momentous embrace, and there is a portrait scene in each novel.

4. In comparing the promenades at Faverange to the wild ride in *Dominique*, Pailhès recognized the great difference and attributed it to Fromentin's tendency to turn the peaceful, subtle scenes in *Edouard* into episodes of violence and passion. He saw this as one of *Dominique's* weaknesses, a tendency to remain on the surface in his expression of emotions rather than using the subtler internal responses in the novel of Mme de Duras. Pailhès points to the similarity in the names, Nevers and Nièvres; both probably reflect the influence of the *Princesse de Clèves*.

5. A. Lytton Sells, "A Disciple of *Obermann*: Eugène Fromentin," *Modern Language Review* 36(1941): 68–85.

6. Barbara Wright, "*Valdieu*: A Forgotten Precursor of Fromentin's *Dominique*," *Modern Language Review* 60(1965): 520–28.

7. Ibid., p. 520.

8. "Friend, my divine and holy friend, I wish to and am going to write our common story from the first day to the last. And each time that a forgotten memory will shine suddenly in my memory, each time a more tender and moving word will surge in my heart, it will represent for me proof that you hear me . . ." (Blanchon, *Lettres*, p. 107).

9. Camille Reynaud, *La Genèse de Dominique* (Grenoble, 1937). Barbara Wright believes that chapters 1 through 8 were written spontaneously. Chapters 12 through 16 (and part of 17) she sees as composed of literary souvenirs. The intervening chapters form a bridge, chapter 11 a brief pastoral preceded by two chapters on the Parisian life of the author.

10. Fromentin became fond of Vaugoin, the farm which belonged to the Seignettes, and which he used as the subject of one of his earliest successful paintings.

11. In her piety, seriousness, and conservative ways Mme Ceyssac resembles Fromentin's own mother.

12. Fromentin once indicated as much to his daughter.

13. "Just imagine that, yesterday, at my house, entering like a ghost, I saw my old friend from childhood, the Olivier of *Dominique*. . . . He left the Vendée, sold all his land, and has retired to die in peace . . . in the remoteness of Bretagne in Finistère. He has reconstructed in the middle of the forest a castle to which he has left its old Celtic name and manoral title. He does not live there all alone. But then my Olivier has never been entirely alone. Always the same; but it is the same moral solitude; basically the same ennui, the same elegant and disillusioned softness; in the end, the same false idea of life" (Blanchon, *Correspondance*, p. 396).

14. "We were in truth the last sons of the Werthers, Renés, Adolphes, Obermans, and Amaurys to whom one can add the Rousseau of the *Confessions* . . ." (Blanchon, *Lettres*, p. 74., quoted from Bataillard's *Notes Biographiques*).

15. Eugène Fromentin, *Dominique*, edited by Barbara Wright. Vol I (Paris, 1966), pp. xxxii–xxxvi.

16. Louis Gillet proposed Fromentin's teacher of philosophy, Bardaud. Neither Delayant nor Bardaud had the close personal influence which Augustin had. Louis Gillet, "Eugène Fromentin et *Dominique*, d'après des documents inédits," *Revue de Paris* 4 (1905): 533.

17. Suggested by Camille Reynaud and supported by Barbara Wright.

18. Not all correspondence has been preserved and not all that is extant has been made public.

19. In the past scholars have sought to identify every element in the text with some person, event or setting in Fromentin's own life. Thus the fact that Dominique had no parents was said to reflect the long conflict with his parents, especially his father, and that the orphaning of Dominique reflected his own sense of being a spiritual orphan. Mme Ceyssac was seen to have the gentle, pious qualities of Fromentin's mother. One must not lose sight of the fact that Fromentin was writing a novel and not autobiography. Characters have traits from people Fromentin knew, because novelists frequently form the character of a given personage from someone they have known. If Fromentin altered the autobiographical reality, it is because the story of the novel would be encumbered by the fact. In reality Madeleine had three children. In the novel children would have been a superfluous burden and might have posed serious technical problems. For the essence of the story Fromentin was telling, they were an unnecessary element. In his own autobiography the fact that Madeleine had three children must have been important. How he felt about this, how he reacted to it, how it affected his relationship with Jenny—these are all interesting questions, but they are not pertinent to the novel.

Chapter Seven

1. He had been urged by George Sand to provide some transition to prepare for his family life. Fromentin may have decided that the initial chapters gave enough setting for the reader to assess the nature of his present life.

2. The novel has been criticized on this point for a lack of psychological truth. Professor Charlton considers it unlikely that Dominique should be slow to recognize his incipient love. There is some truth in the criticism, given the age which Dominique has reached in the novel. In reality the young Fromentin would have been only fourteen. Because he shifted the age of the protagonist to make him more nearly the same age as Madeleine,

Fromentin may have made his subtle analysis of the fourteen year old's awakening seem somewhat out of place; however, the sheltered, provincial upbringing which Dominique experienced presents a youth whose naiveté accords well with the analysis (D. G. Charlton, "Fromentin's *Dominique*," *Forum for Modern Language Studies* 3(1967): 85–92.

3. Arthur R. Evans, Jr., *The Literary Art of Eugène Fromentin* (Baltimore, 1964).

4. "It is in my opinion the best way to know much in seeing little, to see well in observing often, to travel nonetheless, but as one attends a performance, by allowing the changing tableaux to be renewed around a fixed point of view and an immobile existence" (*Une Année*, p. 6).

5. Evans, *Literary Art of Eugène Fromentin*.

6. Maija Lehtonen, *Essai sur Dominique de Fromentin* (Helsinki, 1972).

7. ". . . In this pitiful journey which brought me to the lair like a wounded animal losing blood and not wishing to collapse en route . . ." (Wright, pp. 281–82).

8. "She was immobile next to Olivier, her small, trembling hand placed very near the hand of the young man and tightly clenched on the railing . . ." (ibid., p. 176).

9. "I do not love her, is that clear? You know what one understands by loving or not loving; you know well that the two contrary emotions have the same strength, the same ungovernable quality. Try to forget Madeleine and I shall try to adore Julie. We shall see which of us will succeed sooner" (ibid., p. 239).

10. Evans, p. 28.

11. "After some years the small space where I put my tent one evening and from where I left the next day is present to me in all its detail. I see the place occupied by my bed, some grass, stones or a clump from which I saw a lizard leave, or some rocks which prevented me from sleeping" (*Un Eté*, p. 79).

12. ". . . There formed in me a kind of special memory which was not so good about facts but was singularly adept at recalling impressions" (Wright, p. 53).

Chapter Eight

1. For an interesting discussion of the clash between Romantic and Classic traits in *Dominique*, see Ronald Grimsley, "Romanticism in *Dominique*," *French Studies* 12(1958): 44–57; Marcel Cressot, "Le Sens de *Dominique*," *Revue d'Histoire littéraire de la France* 35(1928): 211–18.

2. ". . . I entered life without hating it, although it has made me suffer much, with an inseparable, intimate and positively mortal enemy: it was myself" (Wright, p. 84).

3. "Do you know what my greatest care is? It is to kill ennui. Whoever would render this service to humanity would be the true destroyer of monsters. The vulgar and the tedious! all the mythology of the coarse pagans

has imagined nothing more subtle and more terrifying" (ibid., p. 241).

4. There are those who see the mutilation of Olivier as symbolic of the fact that Dominique has killed this part of his personality. See Armand Hoog, *Le Temps du lecteur* (Paris, 1975). Those who see Dominique's withdrawal as a sign of failure, as a timidity or conservatism which rejects the new and the unknown, resent Augustin and what they consider his bourgeois values. For variations on this theme see Robert de Traz, *"Dominique* ou l'honneur bourgeois" in *Essais et analyses* (Paris, 1926), pp. 145–66; C. J. Greshoff, "Fromentin's Dominique," *Essays in Criticism* 11(1961): 164–89.

5. "If you believe that I am going to make myself unhappy, you are mistaken" (Wright, p. 104).

6. "Are you sure that you love her?" (ibid., p. 105).

7. "Olivier looked me straight in the eyes, and, as if my question appeared to him to be the height of silliness or foolishness . . ." (ibid.).

8. "That is odd . . . Olivier said to me. Where will that lead you? After all, you are right, if this occupation amuses you" (ibid., p. 112).

9. "Life is not easy for anyone, except for those who touch it without penetrating. For those Paris is the place where one can have the appearance of existing the most easily. One only needs to let himself go in the current like a swimmer in heavy, rapid water. One floats on it and does not drown" (ibid., p. 114).

10. ". . . Ennui is made only for empty minds and for hearts which cannot be wounded by anything . . ." (ibid., p. 116).

11. "Believe me, life is the great antithesis and the great remedy for any suffering whose origin is an error. The day when you step into life, into real life, understand, the day when you know its laws, it necessities, its severity, its duties and its bonds, its difficulties and griefs, its true sorrows and its charms, you will see how healthy, beautiful, strong, and fertile it is by virtue even of its exactness . . ." (ibid., p. 134).

12. "What I wish . . . is that you leave your lair, troubled spirit, poor wounded heart. You imagine that the earth is in grief and that beauty has hidden, that everyone's face is in tears and that there is no longer either hope, or joy, or fulfilled wishes, because in this moment destiny is mistreating you. Look around you a little and mingle with the crowd of people who are happy or believe that they are" (ibid., p. 157).

13. "You must begin again, said he without getting excited otherwise, I know that" (ibid., p. 159).

14. ". . . But to know whether one has done everything he can to become happy" (ibid., p. 164).

15. ". . . A mind whose essential originality was to have followed the ancient maxim of knowing oneself . . ." (ibid., p. 290).

16. "Certainly I do not have anything to complain about . . . for, thank heavens, I no longer amount to anything, supposing that I ever was something, and I wish all ambitious people to end this way. I have found certainty and peace and that is worth more than any hypothesis. First I found peace

with myself, the greatest victory we can win over the impossible. Finally, from being useless to everyone, I have become useful to some. I drew from my life, which was unable to produce what was hoped from it, the only act perhaps which no one expected, an act of modesty, prudence and reason. Thus I do not have anything to complain about. My life is settled and well settled according to my desires and my merits" (ibid., p. 56). See Geoffrey Bremner, "Ambivalence in *Dominique,*" *Forum for Modern Language Studies* 5(1969): 323–30.

17. "Happiness, true happiness, is a legendary word. Paradise in this world was closed on the steps of our first parents. For forty-five thousand years one has been content here below with half perfections, semi happiness, and half means" (Wright, p. 241).

18. "If I had been what I am not, I would judge that the de Bray family has produced enough, that its task is done and that my son no longer has anything to do but rest. But Providence decided otherwise, the roles are changed. Is it better or worse for him? I leave him the sketch of an incomplete life which he will complete, if I am not mistaken. Nothing ends, he continued, everything is passed on, even ambitions" (ibid., p. 40). See Pierre Delancre, "*Dominique* ou la cohérence en creux," *Revue des Sciences Humaines* 36(1971): 373–80.

Chapter Nine

1. "Evidently he believed that he would manage to succeed with descriptions and some psychology" (Emile Montégut, "Eugène Fromentin, écrivain," *Revue des Deux Mondes* 24[1877]: 683).

2. Eugène Fromentin, *Dominique*, edited by Barbara Wright (Paris, 1966), p. xxix. "[Il] finit par alourdir un peu ces personnages du roman et en faire des fantoches" (He ends by making the characters of the novel a little dull by making them puppets).

3. Fromentin writes that he was "forcément très-ambitieux" (ibid., p. 54).

4. "There will always be in Augustin something of the tutor and parvenu. He will be pedantic and perspiring like all those who have only work and will on their side. Personally I prefer intellectual gifts or good birth or, failing either, nothing" (ibid., p. 145).

5. Professor Wright notes that Fromentin removed the affirmation of friendship so necessary to our appreciation of Olivier in order to improve Augustin's position vis-à-vis Dominique. By eliminating the positive aspects of Olivier's character, Fromentin certainly weakened his role.

6. "He did well to warn me. Without him I would have believed that you are under the influence of an unfortunate love. Now I know what distracts you: it is rhymes" (ibid., p. 182).

7. "Certainement je n'ai pas à me plaindre . . ." and "je ne suis plus rien" (Certainly I have nothing to complain about and I am no longer anything)

stress the negative sense and make one focus on what might have been rather than on the pleasures he now enjoys (ibid., p. 5).

8. Fromentin considered embellishing this idea. It is true that Dominique's taste for farming and civic duty are not elaborated enough to make one feel that he really is happier doing these things. Failure to establish this contributes to the feeling among some critics that Dominique's life is a failure.

9. "I am ashamed to say it to you, this cry of true agony awakened in me the only human instinct which remained in me, pity. I cannot boast of an act of generosity, since it was nearly involuntary. True human conscience had so little to do with it, I let go just as a beast would have ceased to bite" (Wright, p. 276). One should recall that the image of bestiality is continued when Dominique says that he returned home like a beast returning to his lair.

Chapter Ten

1. "The wine harvest was made and completed just as before, accompanied by the same dances, the same feasts, to the sound of the same bagpipe played by the same musician" (Wright, p. 24).

2. "The day waned while the peace of the memories was on his face. The shadow invaded the dusty and stifling interior of the small room where this long series of evocations, more than one of which was grievous, ended. Of the inscriptions on the walls, one no longer distinguished anything. The exterior image and the interior image thus grew pale at the same time, as if the entire past, revived by chance, returned at the same minute not to come forth again in the vague obliteration of the evening and oblivion" (ibid., pp. 284–85).

3. ". . . The shadow of the sun which turned around the mast as if around the long needle of a clock, weakened by the heaviness of the day, by the silence, dazzled by light, bereft of consciousness and, so to say, struck with forgetfulness by the protracted rocking on the calm water" (ibid., pp. 177–78).

4. Note that the outings are repeated just as the return of autumn and the harvest.

5. "Madeleine, half lying down, slept. Her smooth hands slightly open had separated from the count's" (ibid., p. 178).

6. "Autumn has an indefinable seriousness and magnificence which gives to the most unpleasing places an extraordinary charm, the charm of regret, the serene reverberation of the departing sun. Spring allows everything to have its flat, indigent reality" (Blanchon, *Lettres*, p. 213).

7. ". . . I thought that I perceived on Madeleine's face a shadow, like a care which had never appeared there. Her cordiality, always even, contained as much affection but more seriousness. An apprehension, a regret, perhaps, something the effect of which alone was visible, had just been introduced between us like a first warning of separation" (Wright, p. 118).

8. ". . . I entered Madame Ceyssac's house as one crossed the threshold of a prison . . ." (ibid., p. 70).

9. "It was a vast house, situated in the quarter which was not the most deserted but the most serious of the town, bordering on convents. It had a very small garden which grew mouldy in the shade of its high walls, large rooms without air and without view, sonorous vestibules, a stone staircase turning in a dark stairway, and too few people to give it life. You felt there the coldness of former customs and the rigidity of provincial mores . . ." (ibid.).

10. "Imagine a very small town, devout, sad, old-fashioned, in a forgotten corner of the province, leading nowhere, serving nothing, from which life withdrew from day to day and which the country invaded. There was no industry, a dead commerce, a bourgeoisie living narrowly from its resources, an aristocracy which sulked. During the day the streets were without movement; at night the avenues were without lights. There was a peevish silence interrupted only by the ringing of church bells" (ibid., p. 76).

11. "Long boulevards, planted with very beautiful and dark elms, surrounded by a harsh shadow" (ibid.).

12. "In the humid wind one inhaled the scent of tar, hemp, and boards of the fir tree. It was all monotonous and ugly . . ." (ibid.).

13. "We arrived at Paris in the evening. Everywhere else it would have been late. It was raining; it was cold. I perceived at first only the muddy streets, wet pavement gleaming under the light of shops, the rapid and continual flash of carriages which splashed one another as they passed. I saw a multitude of sparkling lights without symmetry in long avenues of black houses whose height appeared prodigious to me. I was struck, I remember, by the smell of gas which indicated a city where one lived at night as much as in the day and I remember the pallor of the faces which would have made me believe that they were in poor health" (ibid., p. 141).

14. Both Camille Reynaud and Barbara Wright point out that the phrase, "de courte venue," is not correct for a tree whose growth is stunted only by cutting at the top.

15. "I remember that one saw from the windows two large windmills which stood out above the enclosing wall and whose gray blades, striped with dark rods, turned without ceasing before one's eyes with a monotonous, soporific movement" (ibid., p. 228).

16. "Then Madeleine cast a quick glance around her as if to take everyone around her as a witness of what she was about to do. Then she got up and, without pronouncing a single word, but while accompanying this movement of surrender with the most candid and beautiful of smiles, she placed her two bare hands into the hands of the count" (ibid., p. 124).

17. "Toward the middle of the night, I heard over the roof, in the distance, within sound's reach, a brief, sharp cry, which, even in the thick of these convulsions, made my heart beat like the cry of a friend. I opened the window and listened. It was sea curlews which came up again with the high tide and

went in full flight toward the river. The cry was repeated once or twice . . ." (ibid., p. 131).

18. Whenever Dominique encounters Père Jacques, who always likes to reminisce, he is disturbed. On one occasion he abruptly rides off. The reader concludes that the events are so painful to Dominique to remember that he cannot bear it. Yet he himself retains the room in which he retires just for the purpose of reminiscing.

19. ". . . Like a definitive revelation which completed the revelations of the preceding days, joined them together, so to speak, in a cluster of evidence and, I believe, explained them all" (ibid., p. 94).

20. Another example of Fromentin's use of seasons.

21. ". . . I thought that I perceived on Madeleine's face a shadow and a sort of anxiety which had never appeared there" (ibid., p. 118).

22. "I see her yet, her head slightly bent over her crewel-work, her face obscured by the shadow of her brown hair, enveloped in the reddish reflection of the lamps" (ibid., p. 119).

23. "What I say to you there I realized in a few seconds. Then it seemed to me that the lights were extinguished" (ibid., p. 120).

24. "My friend, you are ungrateful!" (ibid., p. 184).

25. "Having arrived exactly to the place where she had disappeared, I found her at the intersection of two paths, stopped, breathless and awaiting me with a smile on her lips" (ibid., p. 271).

26. "She answered me only by a direct look which made me flush and sedately she took again the path to the chateau. We returned at a walking pace without exchanging a single word . . ." (ibid.).

27. Armand Hoog, *Le Temps du lecteur* (Paris, 1975).

28. "For anyone who pays a little attention, *Dominique* becomes the novel of the wound and the knife" (Hoog, p. 179).

29. The final delay of two years precedes the greatest crisis and her ultimate reduction to a state of surrender.

Selected Bibliography

PRIMARY SOURCES

BLANCHON, PIERRE. *Correspondance et fragments inédits*. Paris: Plon-Nourrit, 1912. Essential study and documents.
———. *Lettres de jeunesse*. Paris: Plon-Nourrit, 1908. Essential study and documents.
FROMENTIN, EUGÈNE. *Dominique*. Biography, commentaries, and notes by Maxime Revon. Paris: Conard, 1937. Critical apparatus of use.
———. *Dominique*. Edited, with introduction, notes, and variants by Barbara Wright. Paris: Didier, 1966. Excellent.
———. *Dominique*. Introduction and notes by Emile Henriot. Paris: Garnier, 1936. Useful.
———. *Dominique*. Introduction by Armand Hoog. Paris: Armand Colin, 1959. Interesting introduction.
———. *Une Année dans le Sahel*. Paris: Plon, 1877.
———. *Un Eté dans le Sahara*. With preface of 1874. Paris: Plon, 1877. Important preface.
———. *Un Eté dans le Sahara*. Introduction, commentary, and notes by Maxime Revon. Paris: Conard, 1938. Useful.
———. *Fromentin, le peintre et l'écrivain* (1820–1876). La Rochelle, 1970. Excellent catalogue of extant documents.
———. *Gustave Drouineau* (1842). Introduction and notes by Barbara Wright. Paris: Minard, 1969. Valuable edition.
———. *Les Maîtres d'autrefois*. Edited, with introduction, notes, and variants by Pierre Moisy. Paris: Garnier, 1972. Excellent.
———. *Voyage en Egypte* (1869). Introduction and notes by J-M. Carré. Paris: Aubier, 1935. Only independent edition.
WRIGHT, BARBARA, and MOISY, PIERRE. *Gustave Moreau et Eugène Fromentin: Documents inédits*. La Rochelle: Quartier Latin, 1972. Valuable correspondence.

SECONDARY SOURCES

ALAZARD, JEAN. "Comment Fromentin a vu l'Afrique du Nord." *Le Correspondant* (1930), pp. 243–59. The painter's perspective.
———. *L'Orient et la peinture française au XIXe siècle*. Paris: Plon, 1930. Somewhat dated, but overview is helpful.

BEAUME, GEORGES. *Fromentin*. Paris: Lafitte, 1911. Use with care.
——. *Fromentin*. Paris: Michaud, n.d.. Use with care.
BIGOT, CHARLES. "Eugène Fromentin." *Revue Bleue* 12(1877): 989–95. Contemporary assessment of Fromentin's paintings.
BLANCHON, PIERRE. "L'Originalité de Dominique." *Revue Bleue* (1909), pp. 726–28; (1909), pp. 754–59. Against article of Pailhès.
BREMNER, GEOFFREY. "Ambivalence in *Dominique*." *Forum for Modern Language Studies* 5(1969): 323–30. Interesting analysis.
CASTEX, PIERRE. "Fromentin," in *La Critique d'art en France au XIXe siecle*. Paris: CDU, 1958. Excellent general study.
CHARLTON, D. G. "Fromentin's *Dominique*." *Forum for Modern Language Studies* 3(1967): 85–92. Comments on characterization and motivation.
CRESSOT, MARCEL. "Le Sens de *Dominique*." *Revue d'Histoire Littéraire de la France* (1928), pp. 211–18. Importance of didacticism.
DELANCRE, PIERRE. "*Dominique* ou la cohérence en creux." *Revue des Sciences Humaines* 36(1971): 373–80. Ambiguity of *Dominique*.
DU CAMP, MAXIME. *Souvenirs littéraires*. Paris: Hachette, 1882, vol. I, p. 350; vol. II, pp. 200–206. Important personal comments.
ECKSTEIN, MARIE. *Le Rôle du souvenir dans l'oeuvre d'Eugène Fromentin*. Zurich: Juris-Verlag, 1970. Significant analysis.
EVANS, ARTHUR. *The Literary Art of Eugène Fromentin*. Baltimore: Johns Hopkins, 1964. Especially useful for study of style.
FERRUCCI, FRANCO. "Fromentin e l'immobile felicità." *Rivista di letterature moderne e comparate* 17(1964): 178–96. Significant concept.
FOSCA, FRANÇOIS. "Fromentin," in *De Diderot à Valéry: les écrivains et les arts visuels*. Paris: A. Michel, 1960, pp. 211–31. Narrow, modern critique of *Maîtres*.
GARCIN, PHILIPPE. "Le Souvenir dans *Dominique*." *Nouvelle Revue Française* (1957), pp. 111–21. Memory and permanence.
GONNARD, PHILIPPE. "La Leçon de Fromentin." *Revue Bleue* (1910), pp. 303–307; (1910): 334–41. Fromentin's classicism.
GONSE, LOUIS. *Eugène Fromentin*. Paris: Quantin, 1881. Good introduction.
GRANT, RICHARD, and SEVERIN, NELLY. "Weaving Imagery in Fromentin's *Dominique*." *Nineteenth Century French Studies* 1(1973): 155–61.
GRESHOFF, C. J. "Fromentin's *Dominique*." *Essays in Criticism* 11(1961): 164–89. Reasoned critique.
GRIMSLEY, RONALD. "Romanticism in *Dominique*." *French Studies* 12(1958): 44–57. Interesting comments on Dominique's Romantic traits.
HENRIOT, EMILE. "Fromentin et *Dominique*." *Revue des Deux Mondes* 35(1936): 572–94. Interesting comments on Fromentin's values.
HERZFELD, CLAUDE. *Dominique de Fromentin*. Paris: Nizet, 1977. Somewhat abstract.
HOOG, ARMAND. *Le Temps du lecteur ou l'agent secret*. Paris: PUF, 1975. Provocative.
HOUSSAYE, HENRY. "Eugène Fromentin: l'exposition de son oeuvre à

l'Ecole des Beaux-Arts." *Revue des Deux Mondes* (1877), pp. 882–95. Interesting comments.

HUBERT, RENÉE. "Fromentin's *Dominique*: The confession of a man who judges himself." *PMLA* 82(1967): 634–39.

KAPPELER, WALTRUD. *Fromentin, ein Dichter der Erinnerung*. Winterthur-Toss: Paul Gehring, 1949. Interesting comments on memory.

KNAPP, LOTHAR. "*Roman personnel* und romantische *sensibilité*: Constant, Musset, Fromentin." *Zeitschrift für französische Sprache und Literatur* 81(1971): 98–135. Perceptive contrast.

LAGRANGE, ANDRÉE. *L'Art de Fromentin*. Paris: Dervy, 1952. Useful general introduction.

LATIOLAIS, F. M. "Not quite a Masterpiece: Fromentin's *Dominique* Reconsidered." *Mosaic* 4(1970): 35–48. Inner Dominique discussed.

LEHTONEN, MAIJA. *Essai sur Dominique de Fromentin*. Helsinki: Annales Academiae Scientiarum Fennicae, 1972. Narrow perspective.

MAGOWAN, ROBIN. "*Dominique*: The Genesis of a Pastoral." *Esprit Créateur* 13(1973): 340–50. Pastoral by analogy.

———. "Fromentin and Jewett: Pastoral Narrative in the Nineteenth Century." *Comparative Literature* 16(1964): 331–37.

MARCOS, FOUAD. *Fromentin et l'Afrique*. Montreal: Editions Cosmos, 1973. Focus on Fromentin's relationship to Africa.

MARTINO, PIERRE. "Les Descriptions de Fromentin." *Revue Africaine* (1910): 343–92. Good analysis of travel books.

———. "Fromentin: essai de bibliographie critique." *Revue Africaine* (1914), pp. 153–82. Superseded by Wright.

MEIN, MARGARET. *A Foretaste of Proust*. Farnborough, Hants: Saxon House, 1974. Distinguishes precursor from apparent similarity.

MONGE, JACQUES. "Un Précurseur de Proust: Fromentin. et la mémoire affective." *Revue d'Histoire Littéraire de la France* (1961), pp. 564–88. Excellent study.

MONTÉGUT, ÉMILE. "Eugène Fromentin, écrivain." *Revue des Deux Mondes* 24(1877): 674–91. Hostile critique.

PAILHÈS, GEORGES. "Le Modèle de *Dominique*." *Revue Bleue* (1909), pp. 330–33; (1909), pp. 358–62. Generally rejected thesis.

PELLEGRINI, CARLO. *Eugenio Fromentin*. Ferrara: Società Tipografica Editrice 'Taddei,' 1921. Somewhat dated.

PITTALUGA, MARY. "Eugène Fromentin e le origini della moderna critica d'arte." *L'Arte* 21(1918): 145–89. Useful, somewhat dated.

REYNAUD, CAMILLE. *La Genèse de Dominique*. Grenoble: Arthaud, 1937. Identifies autobiographical elements.

RHODES, SAMUEL. "Sources of Eugène Fromentin's *Dominique*." *PMLA* 45(1930): 939–49. Romantic novels which resemble *Dominique*.

RICHARD, JEAN. "Paysages de Fromentin" in *Littérature et sensation*. Paris: Editions du Seuil, 1954, pp. 221–62. Sensitive critique.

ROMUS, ANDRÉ. "Fromentin critique d'art." *Marche romane* 12(1962): 19–24. Useful discussion.

SACKVILLE-WEST, EDWARD. "An Elegiac Novel," in *Inclinations*. London: Secker and Warburg, 1949, pp. 182–88.

SCHAPIRO, MEYER. "Fromentin as a critic." *Partisan Review* (1949), pp. 25–51. Biased but perceptive.

SELLS, A. LYTTON. "A Disciple of *Obermann*: Eugène Fromentin." *Modern Language Review* 36(1941): 68–85. Plausible suggestion.

SLOANE, JOSEPH. *French Painting Between the Past and Present*. Princeton, N.J.: Princeton University Press, 1951. Excellent study.

THIBAUDET, ALBERT. *Intérieurs; Baudelaire, Fromentin, Amiel*. Paris: Plon-Nourrit, 1924. Perceptive discussion.

TRAZ, ROBERT DE. "*Dominique* ou l'honneur bourgeois," in *Essais et analyses*. Paris: Cres, 1926, pp. 145–66. Narrow, hostile perspective.

VIER, JACQUES. *Pour l'étude du Dominique de Fromentin*. Paris: Lettres modernes, 1958. Useful collection of essays.

WAILLE, VICTOR. "Le monument de Fromentin." *Revue Africaine* 47(1903): 312–34. Superficial.

WAIS, KURT. "Die Existenz als dichterisches Thema im Fromentins *Dominique*." *Zeitschrift für französische Sprache und Literatur* 66(1956): 202–22. Interesting focal point.

WEST, C. B. "Notes on *Dominique*." *French Studies* 9(1955): 116–28. Valuable commentary.

WRIGHT, BARBARA. "La Dédicace de Dominique." *Studi Francesi* 35(1968): 302–305. Provocative.

———. *Eugène Fromentin*. London: Grant and Cutler, 1973. Indispensable bibliography. Items up to August 1972.

———. "Fromentin's Concept of Creative Vision in the Manuscript of *Dominique*." *French Studies* 18(1964): 213–26. Careful study.

———. "Gustave Moreau and Eugène Fromentin: A reassessment of Their Relationship in the Light of New Documentation." *Connoisseur* 180(1972): 191–97. Important assessment.

———. "*Valdieu*: A Forgotten Precursor of Fromentin's *Dominique*." *Modern Language Review* 60(1965): 520–28. Interesting suggestion.

Index